Teeing Up for Success

Insights and inspiration from extraordinary women

Presented by The EWGA Foundation

Edited by Lisa D. Mickey

Published by EWGA Foundation
300 Avenue of the Champions, Suite 140
Palm Beach Gardens, Florida 33418
561-691-0096

www.ewgafoundation.com

ISBN: 1493519859
ISBN-13: 9781493519859
Library of Congress Control Number: 2013918963
CreateSpace Independent Publishing Platform, North Charleston, South Carolina

FOREWORD

The EWGA has blown the lid off a well-kept secret. It's a secret that women have tried to keep close to the vest for decades – one that has given us a leg up with our bosses and clients, put us on the fast track at work and made us closer to our families. It's a simple secret, really: the power of golf, a game that's been played for centuries all over the world, but still has a woefully low number of female participants in this country – accounting for 5.1 million or 20 percent of the golfing population, according to the National Golf Foundation.

Women who play golf are a rarity, which makes us special. We don't even have to be great players—we are still the initiated. We get to spend hours of quality time with business associates who might otherwise only give us 15 minutes. We can hang out at the water cooler, participate in fantasy golf leagues and share on-course war stories with anyone. But most of all, those of us who are in on the secret cherish the sheer joy we get out of playing this game. No matter how young or old, it takes a hold of you in a way that makes you slap your forehead in wonder and ask yourself why you didn't try it sooner.

Stina Sternberg
Golf Digest Magazine

PROLOGUE

From the Sidelines to Headlines, EWGA Makes Its Mark

Men have long known the benefits of entertaining clients on the golf course and for years, many corporate women simply looked on. Even more detrimental to their careers, women were often relegated to hosting the check-in table at events or driving the beverage cart for their company's annual golf outing. Often, even the local Wednesday morning ladies' group made newcomers feel left out.

I know, because I was one of those women left on the sidelines. Even more astonishing, I had already been in the golf marketing business for 12 years when the day finally came that I said, "Enough!"

With a personal epiphany, I submitted an idea to the owner of Emerald Dunes Golf Club – one of my best clients – to host a series of soup-to-nuts clinics for businesswomen to take up the game. We began with group clinics each Tuesday afternoon for eight weeks, with an all-inclusive price of $125. In addition to rental clubs, each session included a complimentary glass of wine following golf. We called it the Executive Women's Golf League. (Today, it's named the Executive Women's Golf Association – EWGA.)

By the fourth week of those first clinics, the 28 women participants all became friends and began to spread the word far and wide. I soon received requests for similar group clinics throughout south Florida. Within a couple of months, I was spending most of my time helping various women and golf professionals set up activities for the newcomers, as well as nine-hole events for the "graduates."

Little did I know there was such a demand for this kind of welcome portal into the game! And that's when the light bulb went off! I felt an obligation to help women throughout the state of Florida establish chapters for their respective communities and to encourage those who had learned the game to usher in their female counterparts. That's how it all began.

But you can imagine my surprise one Sunday morning when my phone rang off the hook starting at 6:30 am. Dozens of women were calling from all over the country, asking for the nearest EWG chapter. Steve Hershey, a friend of mine who was then the golf writer at *USA Today*, had written a short article about my adventures. He included my photo and home phone number, and it was on the front page of a special section for something called The Masters.

The rest is history. Soon, we had chapters blooming in Cleveland, Washington, D.C., Los Angeles, Denver and Seattle. Thanks to the PGA of America (who allowed us complimentary use of their copier and mail room) and to Continental Airlines (who provided tickets for me to travel around the country), I became the Johnny Appleseed of EWG chapters.

Incredible women stepped up to the plate to provide local leadership in each major city and the media in those markets jumped on this story like bees to honey. Imagine – businesswomen taking up the game of golf to advance their corporate careers!

Within three years of the *USA Today* article, we had more than 50 chapters nationwide. Was there a need for women to learn the game in a welcome environment? Absolutely! And were they taught the importance of the rules and etiquette of the game? You betcha!

But the icing on the cake for the whole explosion of interest came in the friendships that were formed, the self-confidence that women experienced and the memories and camaraderie generated at the chapter level, the sectional level and even nationally. It really has been a true Cinderella story – only, I traded in the glass slippers for a nice comfortable pair of golf shoes.

Nancy Oliver
EWGA Founder

CONTENTS

INTRODUCTION

By sharing these stories we hope to encourage more women to embrace the game and discover how golf can open doors, build relationships and enrich their lives.

From Alice Dye, the first female golf architect to Marilyn Bunag an aspiring social worker and recipient of the 2010 EWGA Foundation's Women On Par® scholarship, this book offers 31 compelling stories on how golf makes a difference in these women's lives.

When University of Miami president Donna Shalala served in Bill Clinton's cabinet, her private conversations with the president were not always about the day's issues and were frequently about golf. A hole-in-one helped Debbie Waitkus make the leap from a corporate office to her thriving business Golf for Cause. Volunteer leaders share how golf and EWGA have forged friendships and offered endless opportunities to grow and succeed.

You'll discover how two women in Mexico are building a team to support the young women in their country who aspire to be the next Lorena Ochoa. Judy Rankin shares some of her favorite stories from her LPGA career and time in broadcasting. Joan Cavanaugh tells of her first time at the first tee – swinging in front of her new husband and his golf buddies. You will be touched by Karen Palacios-Jansen's very personal story and that of so many others who have found hope, happiness and success though the game of golf.

Delve into these chapters and enjoy these women's stories. You will be inspired by this beautiful compilation woven together by a love for golf.

And if golf has not yet become a part of your life, we hope that you, too, will soon be Teeing Up for Success!

CHAPTER 1

Golf: A Game For A Lifetime, A Lifetime About The Game
By Alice Dye

Learning to play golf and being interested in golf has meant everything in my life. It's kept me active and it's brought me wonderful friends. It's been a family activity and a family business. It also gave me confidence and put me in a position to do something for women.

I got started in golf around age 11. My family belonged to a nine-hole club, Woodstock Country Club, in Indianapolis. The club was about a half mile from my house and I would stay there all day with my brother during the summer months, swimming and playing tennis.

I started playing golf with my mother's wooden clubs. I would hit the ball and if I didn't like it, I'd run and pick up the ball, bring it back and hit it again. It made for some very long golf rounds.

The pro shop had a new set with eight clubs that I had my eye on. At the time, my parents were visiting in Canada, so I wrote my father a long letter about why I wanted these clubs to play our nine-hole course. I had wanted a horse and they got me a horse, but we boarded it way out in the country. The club was closer and I could play golf every day.

After I mailed that letter to my father, I received a Western Union telegram from my father telling me to go ahead and get those clubs. "They don't eat all winter," he wrote.

World War II was going on when I was a teenager. Golf balls were duds because all of the rubber was being used in the war effort. Sports had pretty much come to a halt and everybody was involved in the war in some way. I remember knocking on doors and asking for old toothpaste tubes. Back then, those tubes were made out of lead, which was recycled and formed into bullets.

What sports we had were a diversion during the war. Sports were something to do and something other than the war to think about. I earned a letter in basketball on the high school team and won my first little golf tournament at age 16 at Woodstock Country Club. The individual competition of myself against the course really appealed to me.

When the war ended, sports boomed. The boys I had dated had flown planes over Japan. About that same time, I left Indiana to go to Rollins College in Florida. I met a guy from Ohio at Rollins in 1946, who would later become my husband. He was a freshman and I was a junior when I spotted Pete Dye in the student union.

We actually became acquainted on the golf course. I was out practicing one day and there he was. We took lessons from the same professional. I was the captain of the women's golf team and Pete was the captain of the men's team at Rollins. I knew he was *the one* and I let him chase me until he caught me. We got married in 1950.

Back in those days, the women I played against in tournaments became pros. Patty Berg, Mickey Wright, Babe Zaharias and Peggy Kirk Bell played in a lot of the same events I played. Patty actually turned pro during the war and gave golf exhibitions around the nation during wartime. I met Peggy at the

Women's Western Amateur in Chicago. She was four years older than me and had gone to Rollins College, which inspired me to go there.

After I earned my bachelor's degree in science in 1948, I went to work for Connecticut Mutual in Indiana, selling life insurance. I made it to the Quarter-Million-Dollar Round Table in one year, selling insurance and playing in golf tournaments. Pete didn't graduate from Rollins. He was 23 years old and went to work in Indiana, selling insurance in the life and casualty business and was a million-dollar-a-year salesperson.

I played in Indianapolis city and state tournaments and golf tournaments in Chicago. I also played the United States Golf Association's 1948 Women's National Amateur Championship in Pebble Beach, Calif. I wasn't interested in turning pro. Patty, the Babe, Peggy and Louise Suggs were much better and much stronger than me. I was happy playing amateur tournaments. Pete and I were both scratch golfers and we played competitively as often as possible.

When Pete was a teenager and all the men had gone to war, his father got him a job working on a golf course. That's where he first got interested in the care and maintenance of golf courses. Years later, after we were married and belonged to the Country Club of Indianapolis, Pete served as the greens chairman at the club.

We planted new trees and tried new grasses. Pete went to Purdue University and took agronomy classes. We had both played golf all around the United States and we had seen some really good courses. Pete wanted to build a good golf course in Indianapolis. One day, he told me he was tired of selling insurance and wanted to be a golf course builder. I told him that sounded like a good idea.

We put out some ads and got some calls from farmers, but they didn't have any money. One day, we got a call from the south side of Indianapolis. They wanted a nine-hole course built in a small housing development. The guy was a contractor and he knew how to move dirt, so that was our first job!

On our Christmas card to Mr. James Walker Tufts at Pinehurst Country Club, I sent him a copy of the course routing we had designed. He wrote back and said, "I think it's great you kids are doing this, but don't you think crossing the creek 13 times in nine holes is a bit much?"

We learned a lot in those early years. We earned income through insurance renewals, so we were playing golf, building golf courses and selling insurance. We also grew a lot of turf grass. We grew the grass for our new course in our front yard and cut it up and put the sod in the trunk of my Oldsmobile and took it to the course.

Pete started building The Golf Club outside Columbus, Ohio in 1963, and Jack Nicklaus, who was 27 at the time, came out and watched while we were building it. That connection was why, in 1969, Jack asked Pete to build Harbour Town Golf Links in Hilton Head Island, S.C.

We didn't actually have a contract when we built Crooked Stick Golf Club in Indiana. Pete got the land, got a group together and went out and built it. We broke ground in 1964 and finished the course in 1967. That's about when things really started taking off.

Whenever Pete built a course, 50 percent of the time I was out there watching. He would run the big machinery and I was thinking about the land as a golfer. I knew what a golf hole should look like and where the holes should go. I was involved in the shape, position and contour of the greens. You never forget the good courses you play, and because we are both golfers, we always tried to bring that into the design of the courses we built.

I also gave Pete feedback about how his courses would set up for women. Pete always listened to me if I told him something was unplayable for women or that the forced carries would be too difficult. I told Pete to fill in a gulch at the Dye Course in French Lick, Ind., because two holes there were unplayable for women if they had to hit over a ravine.

Throughout the years, we also talked a lot about adding additional tees and offering shorter yardages for women and beginning players. I realized that once it became common practice for golf courses to water fairways, a lot of women were no longer able to reach greens in regulation. They weren't getting any roll in those wet fairways and they couldn't hit greens on a 6,000-yard course. I encouraged Pete to build two forward tees.

Pete became a member of the American Society of Golf Course Architects and later, I submitted my name for membership. They had never had a woman member. I thought it was important for women to be involved in golf course architecture. Now, we have three more women.

I also became the first woman independent director on the PGA of America's board. I felt my job was to help women be successful and to work with golf course architects and show them how to help women enjoy their courses.

Pete and I kept trying new things and every golf course was like a new painting. We don't just have a number of course plans that we pull out of some drawer. Every course had a new design. We also didn't take on more than we could handle and we moved to where each course was being built and lived there during construction. Pete likes to be there physically on site to do the work. I walked the other courses in the area and got ideas while he was building The Ocean Course at Kiawah Island in South Carolina.

Sometimes people ask me which is my favorite course, but that's like asking which of your children you like the best. They are all special. They all carry memories. When we built five courses in the Dominican Republic, we moved there to work. Our son also built courses there and our family has been able to work together.

Now, my job is to take care of Pete and keep us going. I have a 14 handicap and we still play out of Crooked Stick in Indiana and Gulf Stream Golf Course in Florida. Pete is still very much hands-on with his designs, but I'm no longer involved with every course. We still talk about the best yardages, and I still believe there should be two sets of tees for women on more courses.

Looking back, when we got into this business, there were only two or three golf course designers of note. Our timing was good and we've had a lot of enjoyment doing this, but the most satisfying thing is the respect we get from everybody who plays the game. Like I said before, golfers never forget a good golf course.

About Alice Dye

Alice O'Neal Dye was born in Indianapolis and won 11 Indianapolis Women's City Championships and nine Indiana Women's Golf Association Amateur Championships. She was the captain of the women's golf team at Rollins College where she met Paul "Pete" Dye, Jr., following his U.S. Army service in World War II.

Alice Dye won 50 amateur championships, including two U.S. Golf Association (USGA) Senior Women's Amateur Championships and two Canadian Women's Senior Championships, as well as five Women's Western Senior Championships and two Florida Women's Amateur Championships. She won the 1968 North and South Women's Amateur Championship and was a member of the 1970 U.S. Curtis Cup team.

She served on the USGA Women's Committee and was the first woman member and president of the American Society of Golf Course Architects. She also was the first woman to serve as an independent director of the PGA of America.

Alice and Pete Dye collaborated on the design of many of America's top courses, including PGA West in California, The Ocean Course and Harbour Town Golf Links, both in South Carolina, Crooked Stick Golf Club in Indiana, TPC at Sawgrass in Florida, and Teeth of the Dog in the Dominican Republic.

Alice Dye received the 2004 PGA First Lady of Golf Award as the first lady of golf course architecture in the United States. She was credited for bringing forward tees to the game and for "improving enjoyment in golf for the average or beginning player."

She and Pete have two sons, Perry and P.B., who are both golf course architects.

CHAPTER 2

Corporate Golf Investment Yields Success
By Barbara Gutstadt

Early in my career, I wore a white uniform and worked under artificial light in a hospital setting. After a decade, my uniform changed into a business suit. Now after 40 years, I'm still wearing a uniform, but it's called business golf attire. The artificial lighting is now sunshine and the setting is now a golf course in Florida.

My upbringing was very modest and it wasn't until I was in high school that my eyes were opened to the world outside my own hometown. I travelled to Atlanta to visit relatives and discovered they lived in a beautiful country club setting where they played golf. That visit inspired me to someday live that same lifestyle and to learn the game of golf. I wasn't sure how I was going to achieve that goal, but I set out on my career path with that vision tucked away in my memory bank.

Through career changes, discovery of inherent entrepreneurial abilities and my goal to play golf, I began to notice very early in my business career how my male colleagues used golf to build relationships. I also noticed how they were generating more sales than me. It made me wonder if the difference could have been that they were deepening client relationships on the golf course? The answer was yes!

By my late 30s, I was the founder of a multi-million dollar national insurance claims review company. This company was subsequently acquired by a national healthcare organization and I was retained as the President/CEO of their healthcare managed care division. There were 11 other divisional presidents – all men. They often played golf socially and participated in company golf outings. I was often left back in the office.

The time had come for me to learn how to play golf. I've never been afraid to try something new, so I was excited about it. Plus, I had witnessed client-building taking place on the golf course, so I knew that I also needed that tool.

But I couldn't just *act* the part. Sure, I could wear the right clothes and have a great set of clubs, but I needed lessons. I also studied the basic rules and golf etiquette and learned the do's and don'ts of on-course business chatter. Being a mother, I had to balance my time learning about golf and practicing it, while raising a young family.

I took lessons from a local teaching pro, played in charity golf tournaments, played at beginner-friendly courses and asked my experienced golf pals to show me the way. My game quickly progressed to where I felt I was good enough to play without embarrassing myself. Of course, I was also learning the subtle details of when and how to invite clients to play golf.

The day finally came for me to extend a business-golf invitation. Much to my surprise, the insurance executive declined my invitation not once, but three times! I was flabbergasted. I asked why he kept turning me down and he told me that he spent a fair amount of time looking for his ball in the woods.

But my persistence finally helped get my foot in the door with this executive and his company. The mere fact that I took the initiative to find out about his interest in golf – coupled with three golf invitations – landed my largest insurance contract. Eventually, he played golf with me in a scramble format and brought two other executives with him, yielding two more contracts.

My perception that all men are good at golf proved to be false. In fact, I learned that many men do not play golf well at all! The difference seems to be that men don't feed into intimidation. As women, we second-guess ourselves, believing we have to be really good at something in order to participate. I wasn't good at golf, but I knew the rules and was confident and respectful on the course.

On a company business trip to Nashville, Tenn., I was invited to play golf with a male colleague and two of his friends. I wouldn't ordinarily have been invited to play, but I made it known that I was a golfer. This new skill increased my visibility unequivocally among my peers. I graciously accepted the invitation to play, while still shaking in my shoes. But even though I was nervous, I thought it would be a good learning experience.

I knew I would stand out like never before, so I needed to be very self-assured. I sensed that every time I bent over, their eyes were upon me. (I was, thankfully, wearing a longer skirt.)

I knew my comfort zone on the course and tried not to deviate from it. I was immediately challenged to play from the back tees, but I did not succumb to that pressure. Fortunately, first-hole jitters didn't interfere with my first tee shot, which I laced straight down the middle of the fairway.

There was not one mention of business during our round. It wasn't until the "19th hole" when we spoke briefly about business. Surprisingly, we talked a lot about my golf game. A day earlier at our company golf function, I had won the longest-drive contest of 254 yards. I came into this round confident and I witnessed male colleagues who struggled with their game as much as anybody.

During our round, I saw golf balls "foot wedged" (kicked) to improve position. I witnessed "hand wedges" that tossed errant shots out of bunkers. I heard wrong scores being tallied, witnessed a few clubs slammed into the ground and heard a few choice words.

At the end of the round, I realized these three men used this time together to create memories and bond their relationships. I was honored to be a part of their day and to experience "golf with the boys." We built a camaraderie that could never have been created in the boardroom. This was the day that my career advanced to the next level and the day that golf became my go-to business-building tool.

I also reached the conclusion that golf is a telltale way of choosing individuals with whom you want to do business. If someone has proper golf etiquette, can laugh at themselves when they hit a bad shot and still show good sportsmanship, then it's a sneak peek into how they will also conduct themselves in business. Conversely, if you notice the numeral 3 was marked on the scorecard when it should have been an 8, that is a red flag – an indicator this might not be an honest person.

I agree with the adage, "Golf isn't merely a leisure sport; it is the martini lunch of the modern workforce, the buoyant venue where business gets done." Rather than using only traditional marketing techniques, I started playing business golf, sponsored hole-in-one contests at golf tournaments, held golf clinics and gave away golf gifts. The result was increased sales, more referrals and deepened client relationships.

Several years ago, I relocated to Florida. I sold my financial planning practice in New Jersey, so now I had to recreate my business in Florida. I immediately joined the local EWGA and made new friends. It was an instant sisterhood full of vibrant, intelligent women golfers of all skill levels. Many of these women also became my new financial planning clients.

Under the umbrella of Ameriprise Financial Services, I became a sponsor of the local chapter for EWGA. I offered Ameriprise Hole-in-One contests at EWGA golf events, gave away logoed gifts and served as co-chair of membership for EWGA with the hope of growing my practice. Within a few months, I had established my second financial planning practice. And within three months, I had 92 requests for consultations solely from sponsoring golf events. This activity resulted in a rapid and solid growth of my new practice while creating a social network.

My current social and business travel revolves around golf. I travel throughout the world and rarely leave without my clubs. On a trip to watch the 2013

U.S. Women's Open Championship, I stayed in a hotel in Southampton, N.Y. A tournament contestant was in line in front of me checking into her room. While I was getting my hotel room, that woman returned to the front desk and asked to be moved from her assigned handicap-accessible room. The clerk at the front desk assigned that room because she overheard the woman talking about her handicap. She didn't know that golfers have their own unique language of golf terms.

The hotel room mix-up serves as a simple example of something I learned early in my career – to know your customer. Understanding your client base is a key factor in a successful sales career. Initially, I specialized in the health-care insurance industry and, subsequently, in the financial services industry. These particular careers both involve sales generation and each works well when a sales strategy is integrated with a golf strategy.

I take both social and business golf seriously. Of course, no two rounds are alike and the same may be said about a prospective business relationship. However, by incorporating golf into my personal and professional life, it has allowed me to achieve my childhood goal of living on that golf course in Florida and enjoying the game. The ups and downs have become very manageable.

I'd like to share three tips to help you succeed in your career and to create a fulfilling lifestyle with golf:

Tip No. 1: Don't let fear prevent you from succeeding. This applies to your career, social life and financial security. If I hadn't played golf with the guys, I wouldn't have enjoyed my successes. Think about your financial freedom too, and don't leave it up to others to plan your future.

Tip No. 2: Once you make the decision to take up golf, play wholeheartedly. Take lessons with a local teaching professional or find a mentor and join the EWGA. Always look for the opportunities to test and improve your skills.

Tip No. 3: Think outside the box! As cliché as that may sound, it's what has driven me throughout my career. Who would have thought that a nurse would become an entrepreneur, financial planner, avid golfer, airplane pilot and now, a co-author of a women's golf book?

I simply had entrepreneurial ideas that I turned into realities. You can too! What are you waiting for? Set your goals, get some lessons and hit the links.

About Barbara Gutstadt

Barbara Gutstadt, Founder and CEO of The Gutstadt Group, LLC, provides strategic business coaching and funding for start-up businesses. Barbara began her professional career as a registered nurse with an advanced degree in healthcare administration. She transitioned into business and created a nationwide healthcare insurance claims review company. Barbara's strategy-building ability and financial aptitude transitioned her into the financial services industry, where she successfully established financial planning practices in New Jersey and Florida. Combining medical and business skills with the desire to improve the lives of the less fortunate, Barbara established six residential-care facilities for individuals with developmental disabilities. She has held executive-level positions in management, operations, development, marketing and sales.

Barbara lives by the "work hard, play hard" mantra. She plans to spend more time traveling, playing golf and showing the next generation of career women that they can "have it all." Her love of travel and golf has inspired her to establish a new co-venture, Boardroom Golf & Travel. She hopes to provide corporate workshops and clinics teaching women in business golf strategies on the course while offering unique golf and travel lifestyle experiences. This new company will also provide travel benefits for members of non-profit women's golf associations.

Barbara currently serves as director of marketing for EWGA's Palm Beach County Chapter and has served as membership co-chairperson for the EWGA Southwest Florida Chapter. She is a mother of two children, a grandmother to three grandsons, and has two Havanese puppies. For additional information, contact Barbara at TheGutstadtGroup@aol.com.

CHAPTER 3

Golf Came Late In Life, Yet Right On Time

By B. Camille Williams, M.D.

One of the last things I ever thought I would need in my life is golf. But no matter how much you try to plan your journey, life has a way of taking you down a path and introducing you to something new.

My introduction to the game of golf came late in life, when I was 60-something years old, but yet it was right on time. The first time I held a golf club in my hands, I had no idea what a profound impact it would have on me. I soon learned that the sport had many similarities to my true passion – medicine. Like medicine, the game has a unique way of healing you. It requires a developed technique, a keen sense of touch and skill not unlike the skills needed by me as a surgeon. I would later learn that golf, too, would greatly contribute to my personal success.

I was never afraid to try anything new and was accustomed to being the first at many things. In 1954, I attended Egypt Elementary School, a K-7 three-room segregated school, in Mangham, La., where my grandmother was the principal and my uncle a teacher. Little did I know that a few years later, I would become the first African-American female to graduate from Helix High School in La Mesa, Calif.

In 1963, the year the Rumford Fair Housing Act was enacted outlawing restrictive covenants and refusals to rent or sell property on the basis of race, ethnicity, gender, marital status or physical disability, a white couple bought our family home in La Mesa and sold it back to us, enabling our family to be one of the first African-American families to own a home in that suburban community. There were many more "firsts" to come.

In 1968, I embarked on a modeling career and became the first African-American to model for a major American fashion house - White Stag and Pendleton Clothing. Two years later, I would become the first African-American woman to graduate from the home economics department at Oregon State University.

Soon thereafter, I fulfilled my dream of attending medical school and in 1985, became the first African-American to be awarded a fellowship in facial plastic surgery while studying under esteemed plastic surgeon Rudolphe Meyer in Lausanne, Switzerland. This last accomplishment led me to become the first woman plastic surgeon in Contra Costa County, Calif., and in 1991, I became the first African-American woman to serve on the Medical Board of California appointed by Governor Pete Wilson.

As a kid, I loved to watch the family television show, *Marcus Welby, M.D.* I dreamed of becoming a big-city surgeon. I achieved that dream, but unlike the television doctor, I opted to practice in a small suburban town in California. I had a rewarding and successful practice, but that left little spare time to play golf.

In 1993, I faced another first and the biggest challenge of my life – an unfortunate surgical incident that horrifically impacted my life. I'd had a breast implant, which was encouraged by the man I was dating in my 20s. Over time, the implant needed revision. I returned to the hospital to have a procedure that required moving muscle from another part of my body to create a new breast. During that unsuccessful surgery, and for a following week, doctors battled hemorrhaging in my body. The end result was the loss of a breast, damage to all of the large muscles in my hip, many of the nerves and blood vessels in my left arm and permanent damage to a significant portion of my lungs.

Adding heartbreak to injury, my husband walked out on me a few years later, calling me a "50-year-old cripple." Fortunately, my teenage daughter stood by my side and helped me grow stronger. Her encouragement pushed me forward. I was forced to look ahead at where I wanted to go, rather than at what I had endured. Little did I know it would be golf that would rescue me from this very difficult time.

As a result of this accident, I was confined to a motorized wheelchair and forced to use a cane for nearly 10 years. At the time, my body was broken, I was divorced and jobless, and I felt incredibly alone. I later suffered a severed rotator cuff, fracture of the cervical spine bone and brachial plexus nerve damage in my right arm as a result of another unsuccessful surgery.

I worked with countless physical therapists to regain my strength and independence, but I did not have much success. I also met with numerous personal trainers, but most were former professional football players and their approach was not suited for me.

After much disappointment and many long hours of research, I realized that I had the education, training, spirit and mental tenacity to help myself. I made a decision not to live a life limited by my disability, so I struggled to improve my fitness, mobility and physical strength. I fought back hard and pushed myself day after day. I soon regained the strength to return to the practice of medicine and became the first African-American chief medical officer warden at California State Prison Solano. I was now responsible for the health care of more than 6,000 male inmates.

One afternoon, while working on my rehabilitation in San Francisco, I saw a flyer advertising a "women's golf boot camp." My former husband and I had been the first to integrate the oldest athletic club in the United States. That was in 1988, and it was 2011 when I thought it was time to give golf a try.

I was so nervous about attending my first golf lesson, that my new husband escorted me to the course and brought his clubs along for me to use. The woman golf pro, at the time, kindly thanked him for bringing me to the golf boot camp, but told him, in so many words, that she would take it from there. She loaned me an appropriate set of clubs and politely remarked that my fitness wear was unacceptable golf attire. After my first lesson, I immediately purchased a reasonable set of clubs and had the best time shopping for proper golf attire. To this day, it is one of my favorite pastimes.

Sometime thereafter, during one of my many lessons, that same golf professional mentioned that I might want to join the Executive Women's Golf Association. I checked out the EWGA website and arranged for a ride to my first meeting with the San Francisco Chapter of the EWGA, which was a Rules of Golf seminar. I attended a second meeting at the Rossmoor Country Club in the East Bay of San Francisco. A mentor was assigned to play with me. That day, I won the prize for the person who hit the most balls into the bunker – just another "first!"

That introductory golf boot camp, along with the EWGA golf lessons and seminars that I have attended, have done much to accelerate my recovery – and enabled golf to become my new passion. Furthermore, the camaraderie and friends that I acquired helped to restore my self-esteem and confidence.

The surgical accident and my introduction to golf paved the way for me to make some changes. My medical practice went from a sleek small-town plastic surgery office and operating room suite to a home-based sports medicine practice. And of course, my golf attire has scored, as well.

Today, I am also a National Academy Sports Medicine certified golf fitness instructor. I am fortunate in my work that I can help many senior patients. Some of these seniors suffer from diseases and injuries that have hindered their ability to play the game. Through my own golf fitness training, I am now able to help many of them work through their physical limitations and return to playing a game they love. And having experienced physical challenges myself, I can better understand how they feel and what I can do to help them.

Golf is ever-present in my life. I have continued playing the sport and am convinced of its many benefits. I can personally attest to how golf has contributed to my personal success, to my profession and to my overall quality of life. I am a proud and active member of two EWGA chapters. I am passionate about this game that offers new challenges and about enhancing my personal and physical success for years to come.

About B. Camille Williams, M.D.

B. Camille Williams, M.D., specializes in sports medicine, physical health and wellness recovery training for the mature adult. A board certified surgeon, she is certified with National Academy of Sports Medicine as a golf fitness specialist. She is currently the CEO of the Orinda Health and Fitness Center. A graduate of the University of California at San Francisco Medical School, Dr. Williams was a nutritionist at St. Luke's Hospital and taught foods and nutrition at the college level prior to entering medical school. She offers concierge fitness and sports medicine for the mature patient with exercise and elite one-on-one fitness training, as well as total physical health and wellness recovery training in individual and small-group sessions. She serves as a medical consultant to the Social Security Administration for disability cases. In 1991, California Gov. Pete Wilson appointed her to the Medical Board of the State of California, which is the licensing and discipline body for all the physicians in the State of California. She is a facial reconstructive and plastic surgeon emeritus and is also board certified in head and neck surgery. A graduate of the University of California San Francisco Medical School, Dr. Williams was a fellow to world-renown Dr. Rudolpe Meyer in Lausanne, Switzerland in reconstructive surgery. Dr. Williams also earned a master's of business administration degree from St. Mary's College and her master's degree in nutrition consumer science from the University of California at Davis. She is also Zumba-certified for seniors.

CHAPTER 4

EWGA: The Power of the Network

By Carla Washinko, CPA

Putter Pan and the Little Lost Balls, potato salad, a new job, my closest friends and my spouse – these are the memories and gifts that EWGA has given to me. I hope that what I have given to the organization survives for as long as these memories and friendships will last in my life.

EWGA, and my involvement with it, began with the mission of helping businesswomen network and use golf as a business tool, but it has become so much more! EWGA has truly changed my life and the association, as it exists now, is truly my life's greatest accomplishment.

I became involved in the organization like so many other women, joining a local chapter and getting involved in the local leadership. I joined when the organization was the EWGL, Executive Women's Golf League, a for-profit organization. At the time, I was working in a public accounting firm as a certified public accountant (CPA), focusing my career on non-profit organizations.

My company transferred me to Philadelphia and I quickly learned that my EWGL connections were invaluable. Moving to a new city, where I knew no one, my new friends in the Philadelphia chapter helped me find the perfect neighborhood in which to live, became my closest and dearest friends, and became the base of my business network.

Because of my not-for profit expertise, I worked very closely with Nancy Oliver, EWGL's founder, to transform EWGL, the for-profit organization, into EWGA, the not-for-profit organization it is today. I served on EWGA's first board as its treasurer and ultimately, as its president. It was this work in the early years – growing the membership and the base of chapters, and gaining credibility with the golf establishment – that created the foundation for the organization that exists today. This is what I consider as my greatest accomplishment – after spending literally hundreds of volunteer hours each month working with a cadre of incredibly talented women who became, and still are, my closest friends, we created an organization that has improved the lives of thousands of women.

With my involvement at the national level, I found very little time to stay involved in the local chapter, other than playing in an occasional weekend event. As a result, the new business I had hoped to bring to the CPA firm didn't materialize. But, I developed a network of businesswomen who have helped me succeed in my career. I found the next step in my career path through an EWGA friend – a job with a company that worked with individuals rehabilitating from traumatic brain injuries. Then, it was with the help of an amazing recruiter, Cindy McGeever, a dear friend from the Philadelphia chapter and the EWGA Board of Directors, that I landed my current position.

Getting involved in EWGA generates a sense of belonging, a sense of being a part of something greater than any one individual. EWGA is a living, changing network of intelligent and articulate women who are supportive, compassionate and caring. This was apparent to me throughout my years volunteering at the board level, as women would come to the annual conference and tell stories of the support they had received through a difficult divorce or in coping with the loss of a spouse. These stories touched my heart, but I never truly understood the power of the network until I needed that support when my sister was diagnosed with cancer.

I reached out to the chapters in California for physician referrals and for members who had experienced the same type of cancer. Literally, within hours, I had women calling who were willing to share their very personal stories with my sister. Others called with the names and connections to top oncologists. I was, and still am, moved to tears by the compassion of the women who reached out in our time of need.

In the early years and to this day, EWGA has been an inclusive organization. It is not just for working women, but for *all* women. It is not just for talented golfers, but for *any* golfer. Even non-golfers are welcome and we will teach you the game of golf. We welcome all ages, all races, all shapes and sizes. I was never more proud of the organization that I, and so many others worked to create, than when a board member made an anti-gay comment at a board meeting. Alicia Jansen, the board president at that time, immediately and unequivocally suggested to that board member that she might not be in the right organization because EWGA welcomed everyone.

As a gay woman who struggled throughout my life with my sexuality, this singular action by a woman that I greatly admired, changed my life. It was an important part of my decision to "come out," led me to open my heart and ultimately gave me my spouse, Deb Larkin. At times, I know that Deb has felt that she was second in my life to EWGA because of the hours I devoted to the organization, but she is truly the greatest gift I have received through my EWGA involvement.

What about Putter Pan and the potato salad? They're just memories from EWGA events that still make me laugh when I think of them. Putter Pan and the Little Lost Balls was a musical skit the board presented at one of the annual conferences. Sung to the tune of, "I won't grow up," we created a song with the line, "I won't look up, I don't want to whiff again...." It was hysterical, especially the picnic tablecloth Alicia wore as the crocodile that ate the hand of Caption Hook (or was it Captain Slice?).

Potato salad? I set up an indoor event in the winter, organizing the food while the members enjoyed the use of an indoor driving range. After everyone was seated, I picked up a club and gave it a go. One of the balls hit off the toe of my club, blasted into the plastic divider, ricocheted off the divider, careening off the ceiling and coming down behind me into the area where the members were seated enjoying dinner.

Miraculously, no one was hit. The ball, however, squarely struck the handle of the serving spoon that was resting in the large bowl of potato salad. As we all learned in our physics classes, the equal and opposite reaction was that the spoon levered itself out of the bowl, flinging potato salad all over the gathered members. Remember, earlier when I said you didn't need to be a skilled golfer? I'm living proof!

About Carla Washinko, CPA

Carla Washinko, chief financial officer, is a certified public accountant (CPA) and has more than 28 years working with non-profits. In her 13-year public accounting career as the director of tax-exempt organizations at Grant Thornton, she focused on process improvement and strengthening internal controls, working with more than 300 different non-profit organizations. She worked on the design of the internal control documentation and evaluation software used by Grant Thornton, including training more than 2,000 partners and staff on its use.

For 12 years, she has served as the CFO for an organization accredited by the commission on Accreditation of Rehabilitation Facilities (CARF) that served individuals with traumatic brain injuries in both residential and outpatient treatment programs. Her ability to balance client needs and fiscal responsibility led to her election as the Pennsylvania Department of Health's Traumatic Brain Injury (TBI) Advisory Board Chair. In this role, she helped increase services to those living with TBI, as well as for their families.

Since coming to Gulf Coast Jewish Family and Community Services three years ago, Washinko has focused on process improvement, reducing indirect costs and building financial knowledge at all levels within the organization. Her initial focus was evaluating the agency's different lines of business, considering profitability and alignment with the agency's mission. Working with the executive team, lines of business were closed and others expanded. These efforts and process improvements increased profitability from a $1.4 million loss to a $200,000 profit in one year.

CHAPTER 5

Staying the Course – In Golf and In Life

By Carol Malysz

"Golf is the closest game to the game we call life. You get bad breaks from good shots; you get good breaks from bad shots – but you have to play the ball where it lies." – Bobby Jones

Life is a journey with many twists and turns along the path. If you could have some idea of what to expect, it might be a smoother road with a straighter direction. However, there are crossroads, back roads, forks in the road, detours and dead ends. Change is the rule and not the exception. So, how do we stay grounded, especially when the unexpected happens?

Golf has helped me to find my equanimity along the way. Although just a hobby to many, golf is a constant in my life. It mirrors my life in the moment. My game reflects my moods, my thinking, my limits and my talents. It's constantly changing, shifting, adjusting and evolving. And so am I.

Golf requires confidence, patience, focus, balance, control and emotional strength. When everything comes together, I feel centered, calm and strong. I enjoy the beautiful surroundings, fresh air, knowing how to meet the challenges presented by each course and the opportunity to spend quality time with good friends.

I've found that playing golf is much like my work in helping executives and professionals plan their careers and lives. I believe the most successful follow these five principles:

Begin with your vision
Master adversity
Develop resilience
Act confident
Finish strong

Begin With Your Vision

"One of the most fascinating things about golf is how it reflects the cycle of life. No matter what you shoot - the next day, you have to go back to the first tee and begin all over again and make yourself into something."
– Peter Jacobsen

In golf, every hole is a new beginning. As I step up to the tee box, I focus on the flagstick and envision my ball landing on the green. I know that the bunkers, rough and creek are all just distractions and put them out of my mind. When I see my shot hit the green and roll toward the flagstick, it's exciting and energizing. It reinforces my confidence and heightens my vision for what I want to achieve on the next hole. However, sometimes, it's as if the bunkers, rough and creek are magnets and my ball is drawn to land in one of them. Then it's time to adjust, think creatively and choose the best course of action to recover quickly.

Just as having developed a game plan for golf, I've found that it's essential to have a game plan for my life. As with everything in life, change is to be expected. My short-term vision keeps me focused on what I need to accomplish today while seeding my future for longer-term plans. Rather than reacting to the push-pull of life, I've learned to say no to opportunities that will pull me off my course. I've realized how to listen to my internal guidance system about what's right for me.

My work as an executive coach is the result of learning how to follow my internal compass. I realized my passion for coaching out of my deep enjoyment of listening and helping others to discover how to create more fulfilling lives. To be able to hear what a person needs and to help them achieve their goals is very rewarding to me. When my clients develop greater clarity about what's right for them, they're able to move forward with renewed energy and a greater sense of purpose.

After a long career in business, one of my clients was not ready to retire in the traditional sense, but wanted to create a better balance between business, her personal interests and passions. We discussed how she could keep her entrepreneurial drive alive, but also have time for her interests in health and nutrition, creative design, travel and golf. Redefining herself beyond business was challenging for her. To help her achieve more balance, we developed a portfolio approach to managing all aspects of her work and life. Today, she's built a freelance business that focuses on her expertise in facilitation, teaches classes in nutrition and weight loss, sells clothing in a retail specialty store where she also provides fashion advice, spends time in the studio creating classwork and plays golf weekly in her local EWGA league. Her travels have included a recent trip to Central America, where she experienced the thrill of zip-lining her way through the Costa Rican rainforest. Her life is now a mixture of work, creativity, fun and adventure.

Master Adversity

"I've always made a total effort, even when the odds seemed entirely against me. I never quit trying: I never felt that I didn't have a second chance to win."
– Arnold Palmer

Golf is an incredibly difficult game. High expectations combined with passion can yield immense frustration when your round doesn't turn out the way you had imagined it. However, it only takes one great shot to make all the pain and disappointment go away – and that's what keeps us coming back.

Life can be the same way. The results you planned for are never a guaranty. Your passion and commitment are what drive you forward.

When my golf partner of nine years discovered she had breast cancer, the world seemed to come to a sudden halt. Rather than being able to enjoy our Saturday rounds of golf together, instead she faced the long and wearing weeks of chemotherapy and radiation. Previous to her diagnosis, our Saturday tee times were planned as early as Monday morning. Organizers by reputation, we would choose the course for the following weekend and immediately send out invitations to friends to join us.

Whether we ended up as a twosome or a foursome, there was one guaranty – our round would result in adventure. With golf balls landing in trees (never to be seen again), lucky bounces off signs, sprinklers, stone walls, rocks or the cart path, along with wardrobe malfunctions and precipitous golf cart driving, we would laugh and determine ingenious ways to get our wayward shots back into play. Golf was our safe haven.

But all that changed with cancer. Cancer is a formidable foe. No one deserves to have it. It teaches us that there are circumstances beyond our control. Just like golf, it's about staring down our negative thoughts about what can happen. To learn to live in the moment liberates us from fear and releases us from worries about the future. Cancer shows us that sometimes the only thing left to do is carry on.

Develop Resilience

"I hit a lot of bad shots, but you just need to laugh about them, be able to have a smile on your face and just keep moving." – Lorena Ochoa

Golf courses are designed with an uneven terrain to challenge and surprise players. Every situation is different – different courses, different conditions and different obstacles. Each shot is unpredictable, which makes it exciting. We can execute flawlessly and still miss the target. The ability to shake it off, reassess and get back into the game is the way to develop resiliency.

Every time I play, I hope that this round will be my best. At least once during the round, I hit a shot better than I imagined. This reminds me that I'm capable of more than I think is possible. It inspires me to practice and continue working on my game. At other times, my round is a series of mishaps and disappointments. I've learned to stay calm, analyze, learn and move on.

Act Confident

"The Babe is here. Who's coming in second?" – Babe Zaharias

In golf, the wind, a wrong club choice, or someone yelling "fore" in your backswing can all be distractions that cause us to hit a slice or a hook. However, we can learn to have the patience and character to keep an even keel and be accountable for our results. With focus, we can get back to our game plan and move on to the next shot. Being mentally strong requires self-discipline, practice and persistence. We are always tested. However, each test is an opportunity to reach new levels of self-assurance and steadiness. Confidence is built in layers, through repeated practice and sustained efforts toward developing excellence.

After many years of playing golf, a good friend decided to change his swing. With video analysis, several lessons and continuous practice, his new swing was not delivering the expected return on his investment. It was very discouraging to be playing a game that he loved and not realize the results he had hoped (and paid) for. Knowing that he would get worse before he got better, he faithfully repeated the mechanics of his new swing. Through embracing the frustration that came with retooling his swing, his persistence finally paid off. After two golf seasons of practice, he began scoring in the low 80s. He attained his payback. With renewed confidence, he upgraded his goal: to become a scratch golfer.

Finish Strong

"Out here, it's just you and the ball." – Mike Weir

Why golf? Who can explain why someone is drawn to trying to put a ball in a hole with the fewest number of shots? For some, it combines exercise, companionship, beauty, mastery and competition. For others, it's a more contemplative pastime. It's just you, the ball, the course and your thoughts.

I cannot think of a place I'd rather be than on the golf course. Time disappears, the world stands still and all is at peace. I am suffused in a sense of well-being and natural beauty. Still, the walk along the 18 holes offers an unknown ending. What will happen? Wouldn't it be nice to know beforehand what lies ahead and be able to avoid the difficult or seemingly insurmountable obstacles on the path?

The golf course calls me back, week after week, year after year, full of hope and expectation for the best. Each time I return, I start at the beginning, try to relax and release all thoughts of yesterday. I trust my instinct about what is possible. I don't look back but instead, look forward toward what lies ahead. More importantly, I value and appreciate those who are traveling with me along the way.

And so, my golf story continues. I hope to play this game for as long as I live. And, I hope to continue to play it well.

About Carol Malysz

Carol Malysz is an entrepreneurial leader whose career has been devoted to helping executives and professionals understand and realize their visions. Whether she's developing inspirational, life-changing programs, hands-on business training, or incisive one-on-one coaching, Carol's keen insights and strategic focus have helped people and organizations discover and navigate the next phase of their journey.

A founding member and president of the Executive Women's Golf Association of Rhode Island, Carol was honored with the National organization's 2006 Canon Businesswoman of the Year Award for her entrepreneurial and business leadership.

Since 2008, as vice president at New Directions in Boston, she has uncovered new business opportunities and built networks and relationships with leaders at local and Fortune 500 companies to secure career and life-transition services for their executives.

In 1999, she started the Center for Women & Enterprise of Rhode Island and served as executive director for nine years, building business development programs for more than 5,000 women entrepreneurs and securing $17 million in bank financing for women business owners. Previously, she served in leadership of the Rhode Island Economic Development Corporation, where she developed successful public/private partnerships.

Carol served on the board of the National Association of Women's Business Centers, supporting development of entrepreneurial women. She has won numerous awards for her advocacy and innovative programs for women in business.

Carol earned her M.B.A. in entrepreneurship from Babson College and is a graduate of the Center for Creative Leadership. She is a certified Executive Coach.

CHAPTER 6

An Alliance of Golf, Wine and Giving Back

By Cheri Brennan

It probably started with rebar. Yes, reinforcing steel bars got me into golf!

That happened through my job while helping tell the story of the transformation of a construction debris landfill into a destination golf course. During that time, I met dozens of people involved in all facets of the game of golf who encouraged me to start playing. It had been about 30 years since I played, dating back to my college days when I took a golf class to fulfill a P.E. requirement.

Having grown up in a family of sports fanatics (whether playing or watching), it took some attitude adjusting to embrace golf as an athletic endeavor. After all, for someone who competed on the high school tennis team and played on a stellar softball team as a teenager, could it be *that* difficult to hit a small dimpled ball?

Indeed it was! Time to go back to school.

Golf lessons helped hone not only some fundamental skills, but also proved to be useful for learning the lingo, which ultimately served me in my quest to build a niche as a marketing communications consultant in the golf industry. Walking the talk became imperative.

Initially, I anticipated the work for Oki Golf would be a six-month to one-year project spanning the land use and development phase for construction of The Golf Club at Newcastle, in Newcastle, Wash., a few miles east of Seattle. It ended up being a five-year affiliation as entrepreneur (and former Microsoft executive) Scott Oki acquired a portfolio of courses around Western Washington and retained me to assist with marketing and public relations.

While working as an outside communications consultant to the Oki group, I became aware of four local organizations that piqued my interest — along with my investment of time and dollars: EWGA, the First Tee of Greater Seattle, the Northwest Ladies Golf Association, and the Northwest Golf Media Association.

The first EWGA meeting I attended was the Seattle Chapter's spring tee-off in 1998. President Shelia Sampolesi made a compelling speech about the need for volunteers. One of the positions she hoped to fill involved public relations/communications, so I raised my hand. Volunteering was the beginning of a valued friendship with Shelia and many other EWGA members.

PR was well within my comfort zone, but golf was not, so I attended only the meetings and social events during my first year of EWGA membership. By the second year, however, after taking a series of golf lessons and attending some clinics — and with encouragement from more experienced golfers — I was "all-in."

League play became a standing appointment on my calendar. My non-golfing husband thought these weekly tee times were a great way for his workaholic spouse to leave her office. My recreational outlet also inspired him to form his own "Monday Martini" get-togethers!

Along with leagues, I took advantage of several other EWGA offerings through the Seattle chapter, including clinics, weekend outings, conferences and charity fundraisers. Being a believer in giving back to the association, I continued volunteering, serving on the chapter board and eventually becoming a league coordinator.

Another commitment was serving as a chapter representative on a committee called Golf Fore Red, a proposed tournament to promote heart health for women. A past president of EWGA Seattle and a past president of Northwest Ladies Golf Association co-founded the fundraiser in part to honor their mothers, who both died of heart disease at relatively young ages. These longtime friends and golf pals also hoped to bring together the members of the two organizations around a worthy cause and a shared interest in golf.

In 2013, six years after inception, Golf Fore Red celebrated its third consecutive sellout, with a large percentage of participants still coming from EWGA and NLGA. It is now registered as an independent nonprofit organization with many of the original committee members continuing to volunteer.

Golf Fore Red encompasses some favorite parts of my professional work – making connections and building win-win relationships. (Not coincidentally, the name I chose for my business, Alliance Communications, also reflects this aspiration.)

Although I am a solo practitioner, I'm a believer in the adage, "teamwork makes the dream work." Whether being part of the team that has helped Golf Fore Red flourish, or helping a client launch a new service or navigate through a crisis, experience suggests a collaborative approach can be powerful. As Helen Keller said: "Alone we can do so little, together we can do so much."

Also personally gratifying is finding ways to combine passions. Nearly concurrent with my growing interest in golf was a deepening interest in wine. The two passions can pair together in fun and fulfilling ways (think "Nine & Wine")! For the Golf Fore Red tournament, for example, I created a cork-chipping contest as a way to raise additional funds as golfers tested their skills in pursuit of a wine-themed prize.

I've also introduced cork chipping to organizers of the Wine Cup, an annual tournament to support our state's growing wine industry, and at a fundraiser for the viticulture and enology program at Washington State University, my alma mater.

Yet another example of pairing the twin passions of golf and wine was the creation of Golf Fore Red wines. Working with Northwest Cellars, which specializes in producing and distributing quality wines with custom-designed labels, we unveiled GFR's "Crush it Red" and "Chip It In Chardonnay" at a release party in February during "Heart Month."

In addition to wine and chocolate tastings, the program featured a registered dietician and an opportunity for attendees to network. The wines were also offered for sale at the annual tournament, with 40 percent of the purchase price going to our beneficiary, The Hope Heart Institute.

Women who play in the Golf Fore Red tournament tell us one of their favorite things about the event is "playing golf with other women." Early in my involvement with EWGA and The First Tee, it was obvious females were underrepresented in the wonderful world of golf. I believe we can change that.

In 2000, I enlisted the chapter's support in presenting a seminar for women on the theme of "Mastering the Art of Business Golf." Held at The Golf Club at Newcastle, the half-day program featured speakers who offered tips on combining golf and business, as well as some mini-clinics with the course's golf pros, informational exhibits and a networking reception. Although not a success in a financial sense, the event garnered good reviews and is something I am considering repeating with some tweaking.

Those "lessons learned" deepened my interest in learning more about using golf for business. Additionally, ongoing research and new contacts and referrals provide opportunities to write, ghostwrite, or book speaking engagements on golf topics. Nevertheless, golf industry clients represent only a small part of my business.

To paraphrase Scott Oki, founder and chairman of Oki Golf and Oki Developments, Inc. (my second golf industry client): "If you want to play a lot of golf, don't get into the golf business."

Mr. Oki, a passionate volunteer, also introduced me to The First Tee, asking if I would provide some pro bono public relations support for the fledgling Seattle chapter, on whose board he sat as it was being formed. Eleven years later, I still assist with periodic projects to promote awareness of this fantastic program to teach life skills while introducing kids to the game of golf and the First Tee's nine core values. For the publicist side of me, this program offers countless story and photo opportunities.

Fellow members of the Northwest Golf Media Association (NWGMA) are accustomed to hearing me tout not only The First Tee or news from my clients, but also women's golf news. I'm not averse to introducing myself as "a shameless advocate for women's golf" as I circulate event calendars, media advisories and news releases about women's programs and accomplishments.

One of NWGMA's leaders is Tom Cade, the senior director of communications for the Pacific Northwest Golf Association and editor of its magazine. When feasible, he allocates space in *Pacific Northwest Golfer* for "From the Forward Tees," a column I write on women's golf.

I also try to be proactive in seeking out opportunities for clients or myself to promote golf beyond "golf media," especially its philanthropic and female sides. Examples include:

- A ghostwritten piece for a business magazine on using a golf venue for team-building workshops;
- A tie-in to a business publication's special section on environmental themes to showcase commitments to sustainable and eco-friendly practices on and around a golf facility.
- Pitching golf-related topics as programs at civic, business/professional associations, and service club meetings or conferences.
- Joining and being active in select trade and business associations.

- Creating, sometimes in collaboration with others, a golf-themed package for an auction or other fundraiser. For example, I've donated bottles of Golf Fore Red wine to other tournaments, to an auction for the NWGMA scholarship, for a Rotary Club event, and for a fundraiser for a golf course employee who suffered a stroke and had inadequate health insurance.

As a member of EWGA, I subscribe to its mission to learn, play and enjoy the game of golf for business and for fun. As a businessperson who enjoys working with golf industry clients, I support efforts to help grow the game with a particular interest in attracting underserved populations to the sport.

In addition to volunteering with The First Tee, I've had the privilege of working as a subcontractor for an advertising agency that was retained to help the Friends of American Lake Veterans Golf Course raise funds to expand is track from nine holes to 18. This unique facility in Lakewood, Wash., is designed for total accessibility by wounded and disabled veterans. Watching these unsung heroes overcome debilitating injuries to play golf is a testament to the joy the game can bring.

Although I've yet to come up with a sustainable formula for "billable golf," and I much prefer "fair-weather golf" to teeing it up during adverse weather, I'm enough of a risk taker to play golf with strangers and venture outside my comfort zone to learn more about this ancient, yet evolving, game for all ages.

About Cheri Brennan

Cheri Brennan has yet to score a hole-in-one, but has witnessed one. She is the founder of Alliance Communications, a marketing public relations firm based in Bellevue, Wash. Cheri credits a client with re-introducing her to golf.

Cheri's background includes work with corporations, nonprofit organizations and agencies. Her golf industry experience encompasses services to golf facilities and associations.

In addition to EWGA's Seattle Chapter, Cheri belongs to the Northwest Golf Media Association, Northwest Ladies Golf Association, Women in the Golf Industry, ING (International Network of Golf), and is a USGA member. She provides pro bono services to The First Tee of Greater Seattle and serves on the Golf Fore Red™ Committee, a charity event for women's heart health.

She is a past president of her local chapters of the Public Relations Society of America, the American Marketing Association and Marketing Communications Executives International. She is the grateful recipient of a number of professional honors and awards.

Cheri is a graduate of Washington State University (WSU), where she majored in communications. Her "Wazzu" friends can't understand how she could marry a third-generation Husky (graduate of cross-state rival University of Washington). She holds an MBA from Seattle University and is an accredited member of the Public Relations Society of America (APR).

Her other passion is wine, especially those bottled in Washington state. She has helped raise funds for the Viticulture & Enology Program at WSU, where she has introduced them to cork-chipping contests as a fundraiser for charity events.

CHAPTER 7

What If?
By Dana Clark, Ph.D.

When I think about the secrets of golf and building great business relations, I think about the road less travelled. We never quite know what lies ahead, unless we are willing to walk down our chosen path. Life is about choice where we have to remind ourselves that the journey in our career, business and personal life tell a story – our unique story of where we have been, where we are now, where we are going and our anticipated hope for the future.

So I begin with two simple questions and I ask myself, "What if I had never picked up a golf club?" "Would I be where I am today?" The answer is a resounding "No!"

I know that I would have missed some of the best relationships, friendships and precious family time that I would have never known. If it weren't for taking golf lessons, I would have missed opportunities to share my life, laughter and tears with those who taught me the skills of the game, not to mention an unanticipated business venture. I would have missed opportunities to celebrate birthdays and special occasions with those people in my life that matter.

I would have missed great vacations, playing in spectacular settings, while taking the time to get to know new acquaintances – only to realize that spending time together driving around in a golf cart is actually a great way to get to know someone! I would have missed the joy in being part of charitable fund-raising events that reminded me that I am truly grateful to be part of something bigger in life that supports the common good of others.

I would have missed great opportunities to meet some outstanding golf professionals who live and breathe the sport and play hard to chase their dreams every single day. I would have missed meeting some phenomenal men and women making an impact in their communities, as well as in the lives of others, through the game of golf. I would have missed knowing that the serenity and stillness of the early-morning dew under a tree on the 13th hole could bring great comfort during difficult times.

None of these experiences mean that I am a good golfer; it just means that golf matters by showing us the beauty that surrounds us both inside and out. It means if you have never played golf, you may very well be missing your unique calling in life. So my advice is to pick up a club and start finding the unexpected personal joy that golf can bring in your life, as well as the unintentional consequences that can lead to potential business success and personal growth.

Having said all this, I think my story is no different from anyone else's story who wants to push the envelope on a creative idea and take it to fruition. For me, it was a golf idea that struck me more than two years ago after taking a golf lesson. Even though I never really considered myself an entrepreneur, I just fell into a simple idea of a golf swing-training aid and ran with it. I couldn't stop thinking about it, so I talked about it to anyone I knew, and then ultimately, did something about it. I realized early that if I wanted to make my idea come to life, that it was me – and only me – who could make it happen.

I learned early in life that no one really "makes things happen for you." You have to work really hard. You have to put in great effort and time, and you have to *really* want it. In a way, you have to be your own coach, cheerleader and spectator, even when there is a plethora of well-wishers all around you, just along for the ride. Of course, luck has to be on your side and good relationships and networking do matter, but ultimately, it boils down to you and your vision, perseverance and passion to succeed.

So for me, I ended up creating a golf swing-training aid from scratch called the Swedge. A dizzy, land-mine business experience of designing, developing, testing, validating and explaining the Swedge to friends and family, other golf professionals, business acquaintances and potential investors was, and still is, a wild ride! People would say to me, "You're crazy," or "Why are you doing that?" Or they would say, "You're amazing," or "I wish I had the guts to do what you're doing!"

At the end of the day, it really came down to just me – with a lot of moving parts and a desire to never give up. Taking business seminars, networking, hiring business consultants, lawyers, bookkeepers, accountants, marketing, production and warehouse staff proved to be a journey of complex, life-changing and challenging obstacles and wonderful surprises all of which brought early success.

Without any marketing, the Swedge landed exclusively in every Golfsmith Store in the country. I started fielding calls from domestic and international sales people and received early recognition from industry experts that the Swedge really was, and is, a very good golf-training product. So far, I have found this ride mind-blowing and continue to shake my head in wonder, sort of, "What's next?"

Inevitably, I formed my company, Avid Golf, and my story continues – only, I chuckle to myself when talking to other women because "Avid" spelled backwards is "Diva." I consider that an "inside secret," in that, women really can make it in the golf world if we stick together and support each other. That said, I find that being affiliated with the EWGA community – and the diverse group of women golfers who comprise that community – reminds me that we truly have so much to offer each other while still making a difference in the world.

Currently, Avid Golf and the Swedge continue to expand into other sporting-good outlets and independent golf shops, as well as online. Now, it is about taking the Swedge and my vision to the next level. I know there is so much more to do and I am prepared to move forward with a smile in amazement. You see, I still continue to be amazed at how far I have come in a short period of time, but would not be where I am today without a key circle of special people around me.

So many people who believed in me and wanted me to succeed was the main personal motivation that kept my efforts alive, as well as the sheer determination to see if I really could bring the Swedge to life in this gigantic world of golf. Truth be told, I know nothing about retail operations. I also am not truly an avid golfer, inventor or businesswoman; I am simply a person who wants to make sure I do my best in everything I set out to do, while still trying to do the right thing in being loyal to those who need my help the most. Someone once asked me, "What made you do it? What made you want to invent the Swedge?" My reply was simple: I said, "I just couldn't get it out of my head."

What I have found in bringing the Swedge to the golf-retail industry is that people can be truly amazing in giving their time, support, enthusiasm, money and guidance to someone they barely know. I have also found that it's okay to reach out, take risks and to share ideas with anyone who will listen, even if they disagree with you. Ultimately though, I found that I am not really selling a product, as much as I am selling my vision and myself.

Life is really an incredible gift – a remarkable journey with threads of beautiful people woven throughout. In this golf venture, I learned there are indeed, special people – even strangers – who got excited about what I was doing and were genuinely supportive, even though they didn't play golf. How wonderful!

Even as I grappled with day-to-day organizational issues by myself, I felt validated upon meeting other entrepreneurial men and women and hearing their stories. Their shared experiences only inspired me more to push on. I found that they showed the same zest and unyielding spirit and determination to follow their dreams, yet, were not afraid to fail. Sometimes, I learned from my own naiveté, only to realize there were other people who just wanted to grab on for the ride without really putting any skin in the game. It was a valuable, but difficult lesson for me to learn.

While I am convinced that in the game of golf, the Swedge definitely has a place and will continue to expand, I am equally convinced there is more to be learned from my entrepreneurial endeavor. So my road continues, as I go down a path I never expected to travel. Yet, as I continue to move forward in bringing the Swedge to market, I am reminded of the words by Apple innovator Steve Jobs, when he stated so eloquently that our "time is limited, so don't waste it living someone else's life. Don't be trapped by dogma – which is living with the results of other people's thinking. Don't let the noise of others' opinions drown out your own inner voice, and most importantly, have the courage to follow your heart and intuition."

My intuition reminds me every day to look how far I've come, while still knowing that the journey is not over. As a matter of fact, when I reflect over the last two years since inventing the Swedge, I am personally amazed, yet humble. Have I made mistakes? You bet I have! All of them – costly ones, personal ones, business ones, legal ones, and yet I take a step back and say, "I would not have changed any minute of it."

Why? Simply because, I have equally been given great opportunities to share my story, to inspire other women, other golfers, to forge lasting relationships, to be moved by human kindness, to push forward with gratitude and grace, while finding new ways to listen to those who have been part of this incredible journey with me – all because of a golf lesson. Simply put, I would have missed the opportunity to learn about myself.

About Dana Clark, Ph.D.

Dana Clark, Ph.D., is founder and CEO of Avid Golf, Inc. She holds a doctorate in human systems and counseling, and has an extensive background in personality assessment and emotional intelligence. She works in both private and government sectors, providing consultation in talent management and training in leadership development. A native of Virginia, she lives in Maryland with her two dogs, Bo and Luke, and enjoys playing golf every chance she gets. And yes, she always warms up with the Swedge!

CHAPTER 8

The Forward Tee Advantage

By Deanna Alfredo

My journey began with a flip of a coin more than 11 years ago and has evolved into a multi-million-dollar business based on tasks as simple as cutting lawns and cleaning trash out of foreclosed homes in Michigan. Some might call me lucky, while others may think they could have done the same thing, but imagine yourself as a woman in an industry dominated by – no, make that in an industry comprised almost *entirely* of men– in late 2002.

Soon after starting my business, local real estate brokers informed me of a broader national marketplace from which I could draw new clients and encouraged me to develop business relationships with large field-servicing companies. These field-servicing companies represented large and small banks throughout the country that found "regional" contractors like me to take on workloads in specific areas to facilitate the needs of their entire client base. As you can imagine, these clients were not located in my home state of Michigan and the end-user client was in yet another location.

Due to the logistics and industry atmosphere at the time, I couldn't simply walk into the field servicing companies' offices and request a meeting to obtain work. Rather, it is an industry based on conferences. Before I knew it, I found myself travelling to several conferences a year. Some of the conferences were broad industry-based conferences and others were client-hosted conferences.

Regardless of the tenor of the conference, I quickly learned that the networking I desired didn't take place in the expo hall, the breakout sessions or even at the cocktail receptions. Business happened the day *before* the conference officially opened on the golf course as a warm-up to the actual conference.

I was one of a tiny group of women during the actual conference, but I was part of an almost non-existent group of women on the golf course. Fortunately for me, all of the formats in the pre-conference golf activities were typically scrambles. After the first few conferences, I was a sought-after partner for the opening-day golf tournaments because everyone wanted a woman on their team with the forward-tee advantage. Having been an athlete for most of my life, I picked up a driver and connected with the ball almost immediately, so I was very comfortable off the tee.

And I learned quickly not to leave that "forward-tee advantage" at the tee box. My confidence quickly rose in my golf game and allowed me to loosen up and feel more comfortable on the golf course in the company of nearly all men. At some point, I would encounter most of these men in future business opportunities.

This confidence on the golf course translated into a familiarity with the individuals and an ease in a more formal business environment. Most likely, I wouldn't have felt that ease if I hadn't taken a chance and signed up for that first golf outing.

Over the course of the next year, I made sure to sign up for every pre-conference golf outing. One particular tournament still resonates with me today. The conference was held in Denver and was hosted by one of my largest clients. I was able to play a round of golf there with one of the senior managers in my client's office, as well as with a supplier of goods to my company.

The course itself was very challenging and had beautiful views of the mountainous terrain. Again, the best part of my game that round was my ability to drive long off the forward tees, which gave my team quite an advantage for the second shot. But more importantly, I was able to have more than four hours of one-on-one time with one of the decision makers in my client's office. As a result of playing golf that day and garnering a personal relationship, I found myself being called upon for special projects and excelling in the customer service we were able to provide.

This customer service, coupled with a desire to exceed client expectations, put my company at the top of the list of vendors servicing this particular client. Quarter after quarter, we were awarded their highest standard of excellence, which resulted in larger work volumes and a greater coverage area assigned to my company.

My connection with my client grew after that pivotal day on the golf course. It allowed me to continue playing rounds of golf with other groups of male strangers who may have been intimidating in any other setting.

After more than a decade in the business and several years of serving on our board of directors, I was elected as president of the National Association of Mortgage Field Services. I was only the second female president in 25 years.

I mentioned earlier that a flip of a coin led me to start the business I have built for the past 10-plus years. The other side of the coin would have been the development of a catering business. My first career was in the restaurant management industry and I have always had a passion for food, travel and now, golf!

Throughout 2013, I built a new brand, Tee To Table, Inc., which covers "everything from the tee box to the table." The confidence in having built a previous business by breaking through barriers gave me the insight to start something new.

Tee To Table is a golf-lifestyle company, which focuses on travel, food and golf along with some recipes and my cooking tips from golf course to golf course. "Bon Appetit Magazine" wrote about Tee To Table in January 2013, after I had cooked a recipe from the cover of the magazine. The popular cooking magazine found my work to be "one of the most creative food blogs" for that month.

By building the new brand of Tee To Table and networking within my local golf community, I was invited to write a local golf column for www.clickondetroit.com as part of our local television channel. With writing the column in mind, I travelled to Winter Haven, Fla., and played in the Florida's Natural Symetra Tour Pro-Am. I found a kinship with the young pros on the LPGA's developmental tour, as I too, am paving my way to greater things.

In building my new business, I quickly began fostering new relationships with golf-industry professionals via social media. Lisa "Longball" Vlooswyk – one of the world's top-ranked long-drive competitors and a motivational speaker – was one of the first and most engaging golf professionals with whom I had become acquainted. After a few conversations with Lisa, she encouraged me to join the EWGA and I found myself attending my very first conference in Hilton Head, S.C. Choosing to attend the EWGA conference was one of the best decisions I've made with my business brand.

After four days at the conference, I met most of the 300-plus attendees through golf outings, breakout sessions and general sessions. It really made me reminisce about those first business conferences I had attended and truly made me grateful for having discovered my passion for golf. To be honest, without the success I had at those early golf outings in the conference setting, I don't think I'd have the confidence and passion I currently have. Now, I can play without intimidation with nearly any partner on any course.

Recently, Tee To Table hosted its inaugural Tee To Table Charity Classic. This charity event raised more than $14,000 for The Gilda's Club of Metro Detroit, a cancer support group. I was very excited to have Mallory Blackwelder of the Symetra Tour – a Golf Channel "Big Break Ireland" contestant and a contestant on the upcoming "Big Break NFL" show – as our featured guest. After planning my first official golf event, the operations skills I've gained have become beneficial to other companies and those groups have asked me to start planning events for them.

Golf has certainly opened doors for me that otherwise, may have been closed for the last decade. More importantly, the game is allowing me to take my passion for golf and to utilize the skills I have honed over the years in my existing business. It has also allowed me to launch a new and exciting path with Tee To Table, Inc.

Make sure you join me on my new journey at www.TeeToTable.com as I work through all things golf, along with a few other exciting steps along the way.

About Deanna Alfredo

For the past 11 years, Deanna Alfredo has built a reputation in the field-services industry as a standout woman business owner and leader. Deanna has also served as the first female president of the National Association of Mortgage Field Services. NAMFS has more than 700 members throughout the country and is celebrating its 25th anniversary in 2013.

Currently, Deanna is using her business expertise to develop a new brand, Tee To Table, Inc., which focuses on golf lifestyle and teaches women how to use golf in business. GOLF used to stand for "Guys Only, Ladies Forbidden," but this couldn't be less true in today's business world. Deanna is showing women every day how to develop and use skills on the golf course to overcome professional and personal hurdles.

Deanna also uses her passion for golf to write about her golf experiences in Michigan and at travel destinations. Deanna doesn't stop at just golf, but likes to share her dining and cooking interests, fashion, both on and off the course, and a passion for the finer things in life. Keep your eye on Deanna as she chases around the little white ball on courses everywhere on www.ClickOnDetroit.com and www.TeeToTable.com and through various social media networks.

CHAPTER 9

Turning Golf Into Gold®

By Debbie Waitkus

Do what you love and everything else will fall into place, the saying goes.

I had never given this much thought until one sunny Phoenix morning a few years ago, as I gazed out the window in my corner office. I was president of a $130 million company in the corporate financial world and life was very good. I was the mother of two fabulous children and the wife of a wonderful husband, Jack, who continued to court me long after we were married.

As I watched the arc of spraying sprinklers watering the grass below, it dawned on me that despite my professional success, our corporate direction was experiencing a shift. And while I still liked what I was doing, I no longer loved what I was doing. It was the kind of realization that, no matter how hard I tried to put it out of my mind, it would not disappear. In the following weeks, I often found myself staring out that very same window. I swear, the grass looked greener every day.

I eventually hired an executive coach to help me secure a new job – one that I would really love. I also prepared for the proverbial visit home to bounce some ideas off my mom. Mothers know things, don't they? For starters, Mom suggested we go for a walk and talk — and play golf while we were at it. She sensed that I had big things on my mind and she knew that a wide-open golf course under a big, blue sky would be a perfect place for some big thinking.

As we approached the tee on the first par-3 hole, I confided in her that I thought it was time for me to find a new job. I asked what she thought about that. As I addressed my ball, a slight breeze rustled the nearby leaves. I teed off. It felt exceptionally good and I watched the flight of my ball. *WHAT? A hole-in-one?!* Yes! The golf gods were with me. I knew it had to be a good sign.

On the next par-3 hole, I hit another solid tee shot. We watched as the ball landed and rolled toward the pin, missing a second hole-in-one by merely three inches. Mom looked at me with raised eyebrows and an expression that clearly said, "I think this means something."

I knew leaving my corner office was the right move. At least the golf gods seemed to be saying so. Next, I started wondering whether golf could play a pivotal role in a budding new career? I certainly loved everything that golf had to offer, but there was one little problem – I wasn't quite sure how to create a successful business in golf.

After a few serious self-chats, I took a leap of faith and decided to launch my own golf business. I told my ever-supportive husband, Jack, how I was going to work for myself and instead of making money just to be making it, I was committed to a deeper sense of purpose – one that included giving back.

My mission soon became crystal clear. I would use golf as a marketing tool to help women grow personally and professionally and use part of the proceeds from the business to support various worthy causes. When I told my husband the name of my business would be "Golf for Cause," he pondered a bit, smiled, and then asked how many zeroes are on a karma check?

Every start-up business owner knows passion is a prerequisite and I had buckets of it. Only 10 years had passed since my colleague, Laura, twisted my arm and dragged me to a golf course for the first time. Now, I was an enthusiastic ambassador for the sport. I had gone from knowing absolutely nothing about golf to knowing it is the greatest game ever invented — especially for women!

I need to clarify my definition of "knowing absolutely nothing about golf." What I knew was, golf didn't fit my idea of a sport. I was an athlete who had played nearly every sport, including soccer for the University of Arizona, until a career-ending knee injury sidelined me for good. Yes, I knew sports, and I knew golf wasn't a sport. After all, there was no running involved. No sweating. No team camaraderie. Plus, golf was boring. I was so "smart" that when my mother told me there was no driver in the set of clubs I was borrowing that first time, I confidently assured her I didn't need a driver because Laura told me we were going to walk and use pull carts.

I will always be thankful for Laura's persistence and patience in encouraging me to give golf a try. We still laugh about how hesitant I was and how certain I was that golf was not my thing. I had no equipment, no golf shoes and certainly, no proper golf attire. It was also 110 degrees in Phoenix that day and I was pregnant.

I learned a lot that first outing. I learned that men and women could play golf together and have fun. For my first outing, Laura and I played golf with three male co-workers in a group of five. I learned what a "foot wedge" is, but only after one of the guys had me look for it in my borrowed bag of clubs. I learned that golfers enjoy introducing the game to newcomers and making it fun. And, I learned how profoundly golf can enhance work relationships — those three men were my employees!

In time, I learned how to generate business using golf as a vehicle. Golf is a magical connector. It opens doors. It forwards relationships. Particularly for women, golf is a passport into just about any male-dominated environment. I used golf as a tool to propel me through the ranks and become president of a highly successful company. I could *talk* golf. I included golf in both business and social conversations. I truly believe my corporate success centered around how I handled myself on the golf course, coupled with the fact there were very few women who played golf in my industry. Golf provided the segue for me to easily stand out and resonate with others.

When I speak to women about golf and how it is good for business, I share a story about a group of brokers who were touring our building one day. I showed them my office. One gentleman noticed a golf trophy on my credenza and remarked, "Deb, I didn't know you played golf! We ought to grab the sticks and tee it up sometime!" The very next day, he sent me three deals. He didn't ask what the trophy was for. It was a golf trophy and that's what mattered. I had barely started playing the game, but I had a trophy for being a member of the winning team in the women's division of the Mortgage Brokers Spring Golf Tournament. Yes, we were the *only* women's team in the tournament, but that golf trophy rendered immediate benefits. The message was clear: I could turn golf into gold.

Since launching *Golf for Cause,*® I have advocated that "golf can bring gold into your life" regardless of how well you play, or even if you play at all. But, the gold I speak of is not just monetary. It is friendships, relationships and teambuilding. It is quality time with people you care about. It's a way to connect with nature. It is healthy. It's a vehicle for going places you never thought you'd go, and to meet new people.

One very special person I've met through golf is Marilynn Smith, a co-founder of the LPGA. I was in the audience when Marilynn was inducted into the World Golf Hall of Fame. Listening to her acceptance speech, I identified with her dream to pitch for the St. Louis Cardinals. She was an athlete and came to golf only after other sports were unavailable. Marilynn and I have become great friends and I love hearing her stories about the early days of the LPGA. Today's LPGA would still be a pipedream if not for the pioneering commitment of Marilynn and her colleagues.

Marilynn and I also share a passion to make a difference for others. One of the best things about golf is that it constantly provides an opportunity to give back. I'm honored to help Marilynn raise money for her scholarship fund, which makes it possible for young women to play college golf. In addition to being the co-director for her annual charity pro-am tournament, a portion of the proceeds from my book, "Get Your Golf On, Your Guide To Getting In The Game," benefit the Marilynn Smith Scholarship Fund.

Golf for Cause began humbly at my kitchen table. I felt a need to share with women what I have learned about this wonderful game and all it can do for any woman willing to give it a try. Golf has enriched my life beyond anything I ever expected. It has helped me achieve things I never dreamed possible. I am happy to say *Golf for Cause* is now part of a widespread effort and strategy to greatly expand women's involvement in the game at the industry level.

Golf for Cause and three of the nation's most highly respected women's golf organizations, the *Executive Women's Golf Association* (EWGA), *Jan Bel Jan Golf Course Design,* and *Ladies Links Fore Golf* (LL4G) are founding partners of the National Women's Golf Alliance™ (NWGA). NWGA's mission is to increase the number of women playing and to increase engagement levels of existing women golfers.

It's a grassroots effort in which we have combined our experience, data and observations to establish a base of standards that help golf facilities become more welcoming to women. The NWGA evaluates and certifies golf courses that *Roll out the Green Carpet™*. Women can now look to the NWGA for assistance in finding golf facilities that offer a women-friendly environment and do it well.

My husband and I drove past my old corporate office the other day on the way to a round of golf with two of our close friends. We were discussing how much we enjoy playing golf together — a discussion we've had countless times. I glanced over at what used to be my office window and thought of how different and how much better my life is now. I'm doing something I love and everything *has* fallen into place.

About Debbie Waitkus

Debbie Waitkus, speaker, author and business/golf networking consultant is the president and founder of Golf for Cause®LLC. She is passionate about helping others Turn Golf into Gold®, enriching their lives both personally and professionally.

A successful businesswoman who was a latecomer to the sport of golf, she quickly recognized how perfectly business and golf fit together. Debbie credits the success of her business golf events to addressing and delivering what the customers want. A true advocate of the sport, she is a co-founder and partner of the National Women's Golf Alliance, which evaluates and certifies golf facilities for how well they "Roll Out the Green Carpet™" for women, and is a former president of Women in the Golf Industry. Debbie donates a portion of the proceeds of her book, "Get Your Golf On! Your Guide to Getting in the Game," to the Marilynn Smith Scholarship Fund – which provides opportunity for girls to play college golf.

A thought leader who speaks regularly at golf-industry functions, Debbie appears in numerous media. She is the recipient of the 2012 YWCA Sports Leader Award, 2012 Eller School of Management Entrepreneurship Award and a 2005 finalist for the Athena Award.

Prior to founding Golf for Cause, LLC, Debbie was president of a 37-year-old, $130 million private mortgage-banking firm, where she attributed golf as one of her keys to success. A mother of two, she sits on a number of community and professional boards and, with her husband, Jack, owns Video West, Inc., a 30-plus-year-old audio, video, lighting rental and staging company.

CHAPTER 10

Powering Through the Rough

By Donna E. Shalala

My foray into golf came in 1988, at the recommendation of a University of Wisconsin-Madison Foundation Director. I was newly inaugurated as Chancellor.

A lifelong tennis player, I used to scoff when people called golf a sport. With so much time between shots, the physicality of golf isn't so obvious. I have since learned that golf is a sport of nuance. The hours-long game requires faithful endurance of mind and body, rapt attention to detail (slight shifts will turn a good shot ugly), and steely patience. In his infinite wisdom, the university's foundation director knew golf could level the playing field between donors and administrators, and between men and women.

Taking up a new sport in your mid-40s, especially one with such a steep learning curve, isn't easy. Tennis gave me excellent eye-hand coordination, but my inevitable hooks, slices and whiffs as a novice golfer would be in view of the people most pivotal to the growth of my institution.

Athleticism helped, as did confidence — a critical ingredient — both in sports and in fundraising. If you address the ball without a solid "head game," you won't have the fortitude to follow through on the swing. Luckily, what I lacked in swing confidence was overshadowed by my steadfast belief in the institution. My mission at Wisconsin was to take the student experience from good to great, and that required private gifts.

In the six years I served as chancellor, the University of Wisconsin-Madison raised nearly $700 million, and a part of it was a result of my time on the links. I had the opportunity with a gift we received to build a Robert Trent Jones, Jr.-designed course for UW. I'd never make a "major ask" in the midst of a round, but four hours in the great outdoors with potential donors gives you ample time to deepen relationships and endear them to your cause. That was a remarkable sum to achieve in those days, particularly in the wake of a severe national recession.

* * *

During my post as United States Secretary of Health and Human Services, I became one of the few women to play golf with former President Bill Clinton while he was in office. He's a very good golfer and at the time, I had just broken 100, but the broad difference in our ability was never an obstacle to sharing a rewarding game. Golf is a great equalizer; we're all created equal when caught between a rock and a hard place ... or a bunker. The president would come up to me before a cabinet meeting and say, "You know that ninth hole at the course we played the other day? I hit a ball 210 yards and got to the green!" He was so animated that everyone thought we were discussing the Middle East conflict or another topic of global importance. The only negative about playing with Bill Clinton is that he's a stickler for finishing the round, rain or shine.

I was just shy of 10 years as a player when a 1997 *Sports Illustrated* article coined me as the "highest-profile female golfer in Washington." I suppose playing golf with the president earns you a few notches on the watch list. Still, after golf's long history as a man's sport, it was nice to know that the notion of a "female golfer" was becoming more commonplace in Washington and around the country. After years of debate, Augusta National, site of The Master's golf tournament, admitted its first female members in 2013. This is a small victory with a big message about making room for women, not just on the green, but more importantly, at the table in business and government.

I've always sought to occupy leadership positions that, until relatively recently, had been closed to women. In most cases, I was stepping into the shoes of my male predecessors. One of my earliest confrontations with the "glass ceiling" occurred while working as director and treasurer of the Municipal Assistance Corp. (MAC), which had been formed to rescue New York City from its financial crisis in the mid-1970s. They sent me to Texas to sell municipal bonds that could bail out the city, but I couldn't get into a meeting of potential investors because it was being held at a men-only club. With the assistance of a prominent New York banker, I walked right through the front door. No matter the obstacles, I had to get the job done. That's what you call powering through the rough to reach the fairway.

* * *

Now as president of the University of Miami, golf remains one of my most valuable resources for getting to know donors, job candidates and other constituents of university and political spheres. My score won't land me on the LPGA Tour, but I value the competition and camaraderie I share with both men and women on the course.

Competition is good. It drives innovation. It improves quality. It's what fueled every career move throughout my life. To compete against others who were highly qualified for a job I wanted, I had to demonstrate my capacity for growth, for thinking on my feet and thinking big. Without a fierce job market —one that was particularly narrow for women — I might not have pushed myself to always take the uphill climb.

Thinking big and taking big risks is Lesson One in the "Top Ten Lessons for Managing a Large, Complex Bureaucracy" list I created while serving at Health and Human Services. I admire people who take on big problems. These are the ones who tee off with a driver 200 yards from a water hazard instead of laying up with an iron. In some cases, risk-taking pays off by shaving a stroke off a hole. In others, it makes civil freedoms and access to quality health care part of our inalienable rights as Americans.

Many of the core leadership tenets I've applied in politics and academia continue to play out on the golf course, and vice versa. I've spent years making sure that every club in my bag does what I need it to do, consistently. I can't stress enough the importance of having a team of people on whom you can rely, consistently.

And when it comes to going the distance, you have to know which club can handle the job. Some people are like drivers — skilled with big-picture projects. Others are your wedges — brilliant in the day-to-day bumps and chips. Build a team with strengths that complement your weaknesses, especially people who are capable of standing up for what they believe in. Give them plenty of autonomy to make decisions, and demand accountability. In other words, let the club do the work it was designed to do.

Perspective is another benefit to surrounding yourself with a diverse, dynamic team. As a leader, you have to look at issues through a prism. Just as the images constantly change when a prism is turned, issues constantly change as data or circumstances flow like light through every angle and viewpoint. Before putting, we take time to kneel down and read the greens. We observe every blade of grass and every undulation of the path to the cup before deciding how hard, or at what angle, we'll stroke the ball. Listen to your team members and open your eyes to their vantage point. It's how you make informed, strategic decisions.

I urge all golfers to explore what their game reveals about their own approach to career and life. Do you throw your club when you flub your shot, or do you dig in your spikes and hit a phenomenal recovery? Do you nudge the ball into a better lie when no one is watching, or do you accept the challenge with dignity and determination? Pay attention to the decisions you make on the course, and you will learn a lot about yourself.

* * *

My mother was a nationally ranked tennis player who aced the 1950s gender barrier in law practice by opening her own firm. She showed me early on that the only definition of "a woman's place" I need to accept is my own. It's one of the reasons I've always felt comfortable on the golf course, even when I'm the only woman in the foursome. My mother, who turns 102 this year, competed on the senior tennis circuit until she was 85 and ran her successful probate practice until age 91. She continues to exercise and stay current in politics and pop culture. She is proof positive that maintaining an active mind and body promotes longevity.

Golf is, indeed, a sport, and it's a sport of a lifetime. Bodies that can no longer withstand the impact of tennis, running or other high-intensity activities are able to move with grace on the golf course. I forgo the electric cart whenever possible, giving my legs and heart the added benefit of "a good walk spoiled."

While my stamina and focus enjoy their workout, my psyche indulges in the sprawling greens, glistening lakes, turtles, ibises, herons and other residents of our idyllic courses here in South Florida — including the occasional alligator. Year-round golf is a popular reason why so many people — young and old, men and women — choose to live in our beautiful state. And Florida has some of the most breathtaking golf courses in the world.

I love the thrill of playing a course for the first time with the opportunity to develop strategies for a whole new set of challenges. As the cart path winds me around each hole, I marvel at the human ingenuity that merges landscaping and physics in so many creative configurations. Certainly my enjoyment of the sport would diminish if I kept all of my focus on that little white ball, refusing to register and appreciate the rich environment around me.

Several times throughout my round, I take a moment to inhale the sweet, warm air and acknowledge my gratitude for a wonderful life made even better through this sport. So go ahead and take that photo of a momma duck's spring brood crossing the fairway. It will remind you that the rewards of golf extend far beyond the satisfying click of a soaring shot.

About Donna E. Shalala

With more than 30 years of experience as an accomplished scholar, teacher and administrator, Donna E. Shalala became professor of political science and University of Miami President in June 2001.

Born in Cleveland, Ohio, she received her bachelor's degree in history from Western College for Women. As one of the country's first Peace Corps Volunteers, she served in Iran from 1962-1964. Shalala earned her Ph.D. degree from The Maxwell School of Citizenship and Public Affairs at Syracuse University.

She has held tenured professorships at Columbia University, the City University of New York (CUNY) and the University of Wisconsin-Madison. Shalala also served as president of Hunter College of the City University of New York from 1980-1987 and as chancellor of the University of Wisconsin-Madison from 1987-1993. In addition, she currently serves as a distinguished senior fellow in the economic studies program and the Engelberg Center for Health Care Reform at the Brookings Institution.

She was appointed in 1993 as U.S. Secretary of Health and Human Services (HHS), where she served for eight years. Shalala oversaw a budget of nearly $600 billion, which included a wide variety of programs, including Social Security, Medicare, Medicaid, Welfare, the Centers for Disease Control and Prevention (CDC), and the Food and Drug Administration (FDA).

She also served from 1977-80, as assistant secretary for policy development and research at the U.S. Department of Housing and Urban Development and was named in 2007 to co-chair the Commission on Care for Returning Wounded Warriors. In 2009, she was appointed chair of the Committee on the Future of Nursing at the Institute of Medicine of the National Academy of Sciences.

Shalala has more than four dozen honorary degrees and numerous other honors, including the 1992 National Public Service Award and the 1994 Glamour magazine Woman of the Year Award.

In 2008, President George W. Bush presented her with the Presidential Medal of Freedom, the nation's highest civilian award, and in 2010 she received the Nelson Mandela Award for Health and Human Rights.

During her tenure at Miami, she has helped guide two capital campaigns that have raised $2.5 billion in private support for the university's endowment, academic and research programs, and facilities.

CHAPTER 11

If You Can't Beat Them, Join Them

By Hilary Tuohy

Friday afternoons were always lonely in the world of finance. All the boys would be out on the golf course with clients, leaving me, the female non-golfer, back in the office holding down the fort.

I met and married my husband in quick succession, and suddenly realized I had also become a weekend "golf widow." Once again, I was left behind. A firm believer in creating my own destiny, it became very apparent — very quickly — that this picture of my new life with the person I married, had to change.

Having grown up in Ireland and lived there for most of my entire life, you would think that golf blood would pulse through my veins. For a country with a population of only five million people, there are currently six players on the PGA Tour from Ireland. Popular opinion might assume everyone in Ireland must be a great golfer, right?

Armed with a large helping of determination and the fact that I had been a field hockey player in high school, I decided that learning golf would be a breeze — that is, until I started researching how to get started in this great sport. For example, I wondered how to find a golf teaching professional for instruction? Did I really have to invest in a set of golf clubs at this entry-level stage? How would I go about establishing my golf handicap? What was all this talk about pace of play and golf etiquette? And, how would I ever get my head around all the rules?

Thankfully at this time, EWGA had an article on the benefits of the organization in the *Westchester Magazine*. Because of that story, all of my questions and prayers were now answered and this organization provided everything I was seeking. I became an EWGA member and signed up for a small group clinic. Great! I was halfway there.

But my newfound confidence level about my golf game evaporated rapidly as the evening approached for the scheduled clinic. My type-A personality did not like the fact that I had signed up to do something for which I was not yet proficient. The other people in this clinic would know what they were doing, and I certainly would not.

That crowd at EWGA certainly *did* know what they were doing. They had the clinics scheduled so golfers of similar ability levels were comfortably paired together. The women at the clinic were so welcoming and friendly, and suddenly I began to believe I would conquer this game after all.

At a "Nine and Wine" event I attended, I was fortunate to be grouped in a foursome with a golf professional who was a friend of one of our EWGA members. I immediately connected with her, started taking lessons from her following the clinic and she continues to be my teaching professional today. It was all meant to be and the things I worried about fell into place.

Living on the Northeast Seaboard and taking up golf proved to be a challenge. The golf season in New York is short and that nuance wasn't built into my plan to master this game in the shortest time possible.

The following spring after taking my first lessons, I felt I was finally ready to play golf on an actual course. I had spent some evenings at the driving range and visited my pro for a few more golf lessons. Confident I could do this, I signed up for my first corporate golf outing.

At least I thought I was ready until I arrived at the golf course. Once I was there, I realized that I was terrified! I found myself wanting to be that one employee left back in the office. I just knew this was going to be total misery.

But I gathered myself together and forced myself to get out of the car. My nerves totally got the better of me in the beginning and I played like a total rookie, which on reflection, I still was.

Standing on the tee box, I could feel my male colleagues rolling their eyes heavenward as I topped the ball off the tee. After a couple of holes, I settled down. Thank goodness, I had stopped embarrassing myself and was actually making some pretty decent shots.

The major moment of illumination for me occurred fairly early in in this round of golf. All of these guys were not great players, as I had imagined. The big difference was their confidence level. Even though their technical skills were not perfect, they were out there playing from the tips — the back tees — like the pros.

And from those back tees, their tee shots were sailing right and left into the woods, all over the place! But these guys weren't embarrassed about their game at all. They would just tee up another ball and off they would go.

I made it to the end of 18 holes and it felt good. Of course, I felt great pressure during the round, but as time went on, I realized everyone hits bad shots and no-one's game is perfect. Realizing that, my confidence level grew.

It would be a stretch to say I enjoyed that first corporate golf outing, but after that day, I knew I could play this game. This was the first of many outings I have attended and now I just take them in stride. There is no longer stress and worrying from the day I am invited until the day I actually go to play.

And with the goal of playing an average round of golf in just over four hours, I began to see this game as a dedicated amount of time to spend with clients. I could spend quality time with my clients in a beautiful place, getting to know them better in a relaxed atmosphere.

A few weeks after I had joined the EWGA, a friend whom I had also persuaded to join with me, called and asked if I was thinking of going to the EWGA Conference, about which we had just received an email. I had never been to Amelia Island, Fla., where the conference was to be held, and here was the perfect opportunity to go. So I told my friend, "Sure, of course I'll go."

So, we booked flights, a hotel room and arrived at the conference, having no idea what to expect. I was so new to the organization, I really had no level of understanding that EWGA Westchester in New York was a local chapter of a national organization. Nor did I understand there were about 120 chapters involved and a lot of women who loved golf! This was a super-fun weekend and it renewed my enthusiasm to become a better player.

A short while later, I was at our chapter's end-of-season awards dinner and was asked if I would like to serve on the board. Without really understanding what this entailed, I said "yes." Immediately as I did, my first thought was this would keep the pressure on me to improve my golf game and to spend more time surrounded by other women who played golf.

I became the sponsorship chair, which automatically meant I was exposed to the golf industry at large, trying to raise donations, both cash and in-kind, to help subsidize events for our membership base. This opened up my eyes to a whole new world, which, until recently, had been totally foreign to me.

I am now finishing up my fifth year on the board, with the last two spent as president of my local chapter. It has been an incredibly rewarding experience working with a great bunch of women. They all dedicate their time tirelessly to give the opportunity of golf to others.

As I became more familiar with the game, I also realized the beauty of golf is in the handicap system. This means I can play with people who are much more skilled at the sport than I am. Using the handicap system levels the playing field and offers fair competition to all skill levels. Golf is also a truly individual game in which you are competing against the course as much as you are competing against any fellow competitors.

Best of all, golf is a game of constant learning and improvement, as evidenced by a book written by Dr. Rob Rotella entitled, “Golf Is Not A Game of Perfect.” I don’t think any of us amateur players ever feel like we have mastered the sport. There are always new challenges, new courses to be played and different formats of competitions to be enjoyed.

As it is with anything in life, you can be winning and think you are losing if you don’t keep score. When I reflect on my game today versus what it was at the very beginning at that first clinic, I have come a long way, but I also know there is still a long way to go.

I have migrated from the point where I used to be terrified going out on the golf course, to *wanting* to be out practicing and playing. Of course, life gets in the way and none of us ever get to play as much golf as we would like, but I have now made this game a focus in my life.

One of the best things about golf in my life is the people I have met along the way. I now have a whole new circle of friends, network and connections I would never have met if I had not taken up this game. Golf really defines my life in so many ways — in how I spend my leisure time, vacations, personal development and competitive spirit. It also allows me to combine my two passions of travel and fashion.

And in just a short period of time, golf has become the common denominator in how I spend time with my friends, my husband and what we do on vacation. I can now comfortably go play in a business setting. I can also play 36 holes a day during a golf vacation in Ireland. Or, I can play nine holes and have dinner any evening with my girlfriends.

It is a game that has opened doors and changed me from the woman holding down the office on a Friday afternoon, to a confident woman finding fairways and going for greens.

About Hilary Tuohy

Hilary is currently director of projects for Filip Technologies. With 20+ years' experience in building businesses, managing teams, implementing and managing change, Hilary is a strategic thinker with strong leadership and organizational skills.

She has extensive experience in both finance and project management within the Media & Telecommunications industry for both large corporations and start-ups.

Hilary earned her MBA from Queen's University in Belfast, Ireland and a Bachelor's degree with honors in finance from University College in Dublin, Ireland. She is passionate about golf, worldwide travel and fashion, and in her downtime, is an avid reader.

She joined EWGA Westchester, N.Y. in 2005 and has served on the board there since, completing her final term as president in October 2013. Hilary was appointed to the EWGA National Board in November 2013. She also serves as the president of Queen's University of Belfast Alumni Association in New York City.

CHAPTER 12

You'll Never Need A Mulligan!

By Holly Geoghegan

I'm often asked how I got into the golf business. I didn't have a list of goals above my bed like Tiger Woods and I wasn't a standout collegiate golfer. But like many, I loved the game and have always been a free spirit seeking new quests, adventures and an extraordinary life. My motto: Nothing ventured, nothing gained!

I grew up in Rochester, N.Y., a huge golf community. My dad joined historic Oak Hill Country Club in the 1950s. It is the only club to have hosted all six of the men's golf championships, most recently the 2013 PGA Championship.

My entire family played golf. I was the youngest of three siblings – the baby by a decade – so I had to practice and play catch up to compete in our family matches. That competitive spirit as a kid created a fierce independence and insatiable drive inside me to think big and work for what I desired.

My first exposure to professional golf was in 1968. I had just started playing and Oak Hill was the host site for the U.S. Open. Lee Trevino, "The Merry Mex," burst onto the golf scene, became the first player to shoot under par in all four rounds of the Open and beat defending champ Jack Nicklaus by four strokes.

Hosting the U.S. Open was a prime-time event for the entire Western New York area. Oak Hill was the place to be that week. Even my mother relented after much badgering and excused me from school due to "illness" to attend one of the mid-week practice rounds.

A sudden rainstorm blew in that Wednesday afternoon. While everyone ran for cover, I spotted Arnold Palmer on the 10th tee. The King was waiting out the storm under an umbrella with his caddie. There was hardly anyone around but Arnie and me. I froze as if I were seeing Santa Claus and got soaked in the rain.

A local newspaper photographer had taken notice and snapped a few photos. He then approached me and asked if I would like to meet Mr. Palmer. I shook my wet head and said, "Yes sir!" Arnie signed my autograph book. The next morning, the photos appeared on the front page of the newspaper, much to the amazement of my teachers. So much for my illness, but I had definitely caught the golf "bug." *Have you ever had a defining moment like this?*

I learned to play golf under the tutelage of two gifted instructors, Jack Lumpkin, Sr. and Craig Harmon, head professionals at Oak Hill at the time and both ranked in the top 50 in the country. Craig is part of the famous Harmon family of golf instructors including father, Claude, and brothers, Butch, Dick and Billy.

Craig was ahead of his time with his junior golf program. He put great emphasis on the etiquette and rules of the game. In order to receive your junior playing tag, you had to pass a 50-question rules test. I was driven to learn and studied the USGA rules book until I could recite it in my sleep. My knowledge of, and respect for, the rules and the integrity of the game was ingrained in those early days. It also formed my appreciation for "calling it on yourself" and having integrity in life.

As an accomplished junior golfer, I won a number of junior events including the junior club championship, and played on the boys' high school golf team.

Golf, however, was only one of my passions. I was an all-around athlete and participated in a variety of team and individual sports. Being a competitive athlete helped me to balance schoolwork with practice and to develop discipline, which is a staple in my life.

I attended Allegheny College in Pennsylvania, a nationally ranked liberal arts NCAA Division III college. Allegheny placed more emphasis on its academic programs than sports at that time. So I hung up my clubs, focused on my studies, majored in history and got a great education. This included honors for an internship I designed working for the Glacier Natural History Association in Glacier National Park in Montana.

Returning to Rochester to start my career, I realized I missed playing golf. I joined Locust Hill Country Club, the host site for the LPGA Rochester International for more than 30 years, and started my career in advertising sales. I soon discovered that being able to entertain clients on the golf course and "talk shop"was definitely an advantage. I began to appreciate, from a business perspective, how fortunate I was to be a female who could play good golf and tee it up with "the guys."

While many of my friends were choosing traditional corporate paths, I was seeking freedom and flexibility. My parents hoped that I would choose the more stable corporate route, but entrepreneurship was in my blood. You name it, I had sold it growing up: Girl Scout cookies, magazines, house plants. I babysat and mowed lawns – anything to make a buck. My dad was a sales executive and the proverbial "apple didn't fall far from the tree."

At 23, I started an advertising and graphic design business, which I ran successfully for seven years. During that time, I volunteered at the Rochester International and watched Nancy Lopez and other great players from inside the ropes. I began to get this gnawing feeling that perhaps I had missed my calling to play professional golf.

My father retired and my parents moved to Florida. I began making annual trips south for the holidays and was getting more obsessed with golf. During the winter of 1989, I had my "Aha moment" while watching the broadcast of the LPGA Nabisco Dinah Shore from picture-perfect Palm Springs. Staring at grey skies and knee-deep snowdrifts outside my living room window in Rochester, my inner voice screamed, "This sucks!" I decided in that moment that I was going to get a job in the golf business. *Have you ever gotten that nudge? Did you ignore it or act on it?*

Several things lined up synergistically that summer. The U.S. Open was being played at Oak Hill again. I attended the Rolex Dinner of Champions and was introduced to some key golf VIPs. Two weeks later, the LPGA was back in town. Through a concerted effort and more networking, I met Bill Blue, the new commissioner of the LPGA.

As it turned out, the LPGA was seeking to hire a director of communications. I sent a uniquely written and designed resume in hopes of standing out. It worked. After several months and a series of interviews, I was hired. Within six weeks, I sold my business and my house, said good-bye to friends and family, moved to Daytona Beach, Fla., and began my dream job at the LPGA on Jan. 2, 1990. *You don't always have to know the how, just have a strong WHY!*

Later that month, I attended my first PGA Merchandise Show in Orlando – the "Super Bowl" of the golf industry, where manufacturers and hopeful entrepreneurs exhibit their products and services. There were only a handful of women walking the floors of the Orlando Convention Center in the early 1990s and very few in management positions or as business owners.

One of them, my good friend Nancy Oliver, was the founder of the Executive Women's Golf Association. Both of us were born under the sign of Sagittarius and I fondly referred to her as my "twin sister of a different mother." Nancy and I had many long supportive conversations about the future of women in golf back then. The EWGA is her legacy and has introduced the game to thousands of women across the country. I am proud to have been a part of that growth, mentoring some along the way.

In 1992, my entrepreneurial spirit surfaced again. I launched Golf Marketing Services, and braved a brand new world as a female consultant in the golf industry. Since then, I have worked with some of the top teaching professionals, course architects, entrepreneurs, CEOs and visionaries in golf, both nationally and internationally. I host and produce an award-winning golf radio talk show and have interviewed many icons in golf including Tiger Woods. More than 20 years later, the journey has been much more than a dream come true.

There have been many people who have guided me, inspired me and taught me valuable lessons throughout the years. Quotes inspire and motivate me, especially from successful women. One of my favorite quotes is by Marianne Williamson, author, activist and lecturer: "Our deepest fear is not that we are inadequate. Our deepest fear is that we are powerful beyond measure."

In my 20s, I frequently played golf with a guy named Art, a single-digit golfer and successful advertising executive. One day as we stood on the tee of a par 3, I asked him how many hole-in-ones he had made in his life? He said, "Seven." I kiddingly replied, "Art, you're ruining the odds for the rest of us." He then asked quizzically, "Holly, what do you think about when you tee your ball up on a par 3?" I said, "I think about hitting it close." Art retorted, "I think about putting the ball in the cup." Bingo! *Be clear about your goals, your intentions and the outcomes you desire.*

Family has also been a great source of support and inspiration. My mother and I played in many mother-daughter tournaments. She had a machine-like swing and rarely missed a fairway. Her favorite player was Tom Watson. Sadly, she succumbed to Parkinson's disease in 1997 at age 74. My mother showed me courage, determination and grace in the face of an illness that currently has no cure. Thankfully, actor Michael J. Fox, actor, activist, and avid golfer whom I've had the privilege of meeting and interviewing, is aggressively making strides through his Foundation for Parkinson's Research to find one!

It's never too late to do what calls you! Follow your true north. Seize your inner "golf star." Although I decided not to become a professional golfer, I combined my love for golf and business and created my own fairway of dreams. As Dory says in Finding Nemo, "Just keep swimming!"

Lastly, my father gave me the greatest gift of all – my first golf lesson! Dad passed away in 2012 – 90 years young. He was my greatest cheerleader, adviser and friend. I miss him dearly. Thanks for everything, Dad. You taught me how to live life on purpose and if you do it right, you'll never need a mulligan.

About Holly Geoghegan

Holly Geoghegan (Gey-gan) is president of Golf Marketing Services, a marketing, public relations and business development consulting company.

For over 20 years, Holly "G!" as she is known in the industry, has continually used her creativity, energy and strategic thinking to produce successful marketing campaigns for her clients. GOLFWEEK named her one of the Top 25 "Women in Golf."

Geoghegan has worked with major manufacturers such as Taylor Made, Callaway, Tiger Shark, F2 and Aldila to name a few. Her strength is taking start-ups and developing them into notable products, services and brands.

Geoghegan has been a pioneer in leading the golf industry into the world of digital media. Geoghegan was a founding partner in iGOLF, the first comprehensive golf website launched in 1994. She served as Chief Marketing Officer for LiquidGolf.com, one of the first ecommerce golf sites and consulted with Golf.com building one of the "Best URLs in Golf" which was acquired by Time Inc. (2006). She consulted on the conceptual development of the Golf Channel and is a former director of communications for the LPGA.

Geoghegan is a founding member and advisory board member of the International Network of Golf. She belongs to the Golf Writers Association of America and is the host and producer of her own award-winning golf talk radio show, the Golf Insiders, on Clear Channel and iHeart Radio.

In her spare time, Geoghegan works with Canine Caring Therapy Dogs and READing Paws in Florida. She volunteered for five years as a classroom leader for Landmark Education – a global leadership program.

When the golf gods permit, she hits the links and carries a nine handicap.

For more visit www.golfmarketinginc.com.

CHAPTER 13

My Business and Life On the Back Nine

By Jacqueline Jones

Golf is my flame – that spark that motivates me to act when I might not otherwise feel like it. I sometimes think of my life in terms of a round of golf. In this analogy, each hole is comparable to a five-year life span.

Right now, I'm in the middle of "the back nine." My back nine started at age 45. Many professional women "make the turn" at about that time – reaching the apex of our professional careers. We make good salaries. We have earned professional respect. We have challenging, yet fulfilling positions and can enjoy some of the benefits of our hard work.

At 45, I was a very successful information technology (IT) consultant and educator, but as I started the back nine, my life perspective began to change. During the "tenth-hole" years of my life – from ages 45-49 – I began to feel the mental and physical fatigue from my years of climbing corporate ladders.

I didn't know if I wanted to fight the battle it would take to move to upper-level corporate success. I questioned if it was worth the effort or if it was even possible. I wondered if it was the best use of my energy, given my personal values at this point in time. I was "making the turn" in my life. My entire "tenth-hole" span had focused on questioning the direction I really wanted to be headed in completing my life's round.

By the 11th hole, from ages 50-54, some major hazards in the fairway of life required me to rethink the strategy I had planned off the tee. First, the work world was changing. Companies were downsizing both jobs and salaries. With my current IT skill set, this had not yet affected me, but I knew that could change any time.

The stress and fatigue of maintaining a high-tech career had also begun to take its toll on me physically. I exercised less, slept less, gained weight and my arthritis continued to progress. Then, the doctor recommended knee replacement surgery. After avoiding the corporate fairway bunkers, I had landed right smack in the middle of the aging-injuries rough. I was reluctant to take the surgery stroke just to get back in the fairway. I felt this was not a solution to the real problem.

So, I went back to school, taking wellness and kinesiology courses to learn more about arthritis. I learned that I could probably minimize my losses by taking a conservative approach – like just hitting my ball straight back into the fairway from the trees. I went on to earn a second bachelor's degree in kinesiology – the study of muscular movement, especially the mechanics of human motion.

I had quit my job as an IT Enterprise Architecture instructor/consultant in order to complete my final college courses in this new field. I earned professional certifications as a personal trainer, as a health fitness instructor and as a strength and conditioning specialist. I also started working part time as a personal trainer for three different fitness facilities. My 30-year IT career had conditioned me to juggling multiple work tasks and continuing education. I birdied the 11th hole and was headed in a new direction, although unsure where it would lead.

From ages 55-59, my 12th hole, I embraced my second career profession by working to develop my expertise through education, professional development and practice. My time was more flexible, so I decided to take up golf again. As a casual golfer who had learned the game 25 years earlier, I played on public courses and never took lessons. I had played courses on the south side of Chicago with whomever the starter paired me. I joined a group of men and women who played together every two weeks and took a golf trip to Florida every February. Number 12 was a definite par, but I never guessed that No. 13 would be "the good, the bad and the ugly."

After I moved to the suburbs, my work schedule made it difficult to maintain my golf friendships – so I didn't play for many years. I didn't know anyone in my area with whom to play golf, but I often went to a local course and played as a single.

One day in the parking lot, a woman told me about the EWGA. A few weeks later in that same parking lot, I saw a group of women who were there to play golf. Some of the women smiled at me and said hello. They invited me to play with their local EWGA Friday-night league and I have been playing with that group ever since! This group's embodiment of the EWGA's stated principles helped me to "follow my flame." And I have sponsored my local EWGA chapter for three years for two reasons: because of my love for golf and because of the initial welcome I received from those EWGA members.

But arthritis made golf the second time around much more challenging. Arthritic knees and hips limit golf-specific movements. My body wasn't physically doing what I wanted it to do. So I started studying golf fitness and biomechanics. Professional golfers like Tiger Woods and Annika Sorenstam demonstrated the value of golf-specific physical fitness. Athletes in other sports have long understood the value of training programs that are specific to the requirements of their sport and tailored to target their personal physical strengths and weaknesses. Golfers are just beginning to utilize personalized, sport-specific physical training.

As I grew professionally, it became apparent that the same "glass walls and ceilings" existed in this profession as in my previous profession. I do not look like most people's image of an expert fitness trainer. I am not young, male, physically trim, athletic or white. And, just as in my previous career, I learned that people made immediate judgments when they first saw me. After working with me for a while, they learned that I could really help them.

Golf culture reflects our national culture and our business culture. It is organized by socio-economic status, gender, age and race. Groups organize by basic family units (regular foursomes), by extended family units (regular playing groups), by social communities or tribes (leagues) and by common interest communities or nations (associations). If someone does not fit the profile of a typical member of one of those groups, it is very difficult to participate in activities with that group, much less to become a member. Between some individuals, these barriers may not exist or may dissolve over time through familiarity. This has often been my experience.

I am "mature" and an "older adult" (the current politically correct terms for "senior citizen"). I am female with an extremely short haircut. I am over ideal weight with severe osteoarthritis and with posture marred by scoliosis. My career focus is technical and quantitative. Oh yes, I'm also Black. That is why I found my welcome into the Friday night EWGA league a pleasant surprise.

It was also part of my motivation for starting my golf fitness business. I developed business relationships with leaders in the field: the Titleist Performance Institute (TPI), K-Motion Interactive (KMI) and Advanced Motion Measurement (AMM3D). They have worked with me and encouraged me in my second career.

Then, just as things began to gain momentum, life had another surprise for me: a pancreatic tumor. At age 63 - approaching the 13th green - my golf revival was stopped cold by surgery. The surgery cut a 12-inch, arc incision through all of my major abdominal muscles – critical core muscles for the golf swing. It was like hitting my ball into the middle of a water hazard. I had to regroup, take the strokes and try to recover.

While recovering physically from the surgery, my business has been on hiatus, but I have continued to build my golf biomechanics expertise and credentials. In addition to earning advanced certifications from TPI, KMI, and

AMM3D, I have forged partnerships with local golf pros. The 13th hole was a challenging double bogey, but I'm still on the course.

I'm now 65. I started this hole with a long, straight drive down the middle of the fairway. My major programs at two park districts – corporate injury prevention and strength training for mature adults – have shown effectiveness with many participants. I have earned national recognition as a speaker and educator at national fitness industry conferences. I've started my second year as a master's degree candidate in biomechanics. My thesis research is on techniques for training efficient golf movement patterns. This could be a birdie or eagle hole!

I started a new business to share with others what I've learned about moving the body more effectively for fitness, golf and in activities of daily living. My greatest joy comes when I see "the light bulb go on" with clients and students. Initially, many thought they already knew how to perform a movement. Others weren't interested in exercises or muscles. But in a short time, I was able to demonstrate how to "master their movement."

The magic moment comes when they automatically corrected a body movement to make it feel better and work better. They learned my concept of "The Five Fs: Function, Form, Feel, Focus and Fudges," and how to use those techniques to improve their posture, strength and movement. They learn to "feel the function." Many learn they had not been doing what they thought they were doing with their bodies.

For golf, this focus is different from swing training and from generic golf exercises. The Five Fs apply to golf movements in very specific ways and complement golf-swing instruction. Personalized golf fitness can help golfers play better and longer, but they have to be open-minded and motivated by personal golf goals or fitness needs – just as I was. My flame is golf. My desire to play golf motivated me to change careers, to manage my health and fitness, to continue my education, and to start a business.

My business on the back nine is Jacque Jones Fitness. My website offers education and training to improve basic posture, muscles and movement, and insight on golf-specific applications. I will share with, and learn from, fellow EWGA members in an EWGA blog focusing on golf fitness. I welcome all input from fellow EWGA members interested in promoting golf-specific fitness for women. As I continue on the 14th hole of my life – re-launching Jacque Jones Fitness – I invite all golf enthusiasts to please join me on "my back nine!"

About Jacque Jones

After establishing her second career in fitness as a kinesiologist, Jones returned to golf after taking off 12 years. She discovered TPI's golf fitness research while looking for golf-specific physical conditioning activities for her personal workouts. As an engineer and a kinesiologist, the TPI approach made so much sense that Jones is now a TPI-Certified Golf Fitness Instructor (CGFI) and a K-VEST TPI 3D-L2 Certified Instructor.

As a personal trainer at two fitness clubs, Jones assesses and trains individual clients, conducts member seminars, designs and implements special programs for corporate injury prevention and for participants of all fitness levels, including those with chronic conditions.

She presents at national conferences such as Club Industry on the Personal Training and Special Populations tracks.

She has earned a bachelor's degree in industrial engineering and operations research and an MBA in public accounting, both from Cornell University. In her second career, she has earned a bachelor's degree in kinesiology-exercise science from Elmhurst College and is currently a second-year master's degree candidate in kinesiology-biomechanics at Illinois State University.

Her additional professional fitness certifications include: National Strength and Conditioning Associated (NSCA)- Certified Strength and Conditioning Specialist (CSCS); American Council on Exercise (ACE) certified –Personal Trainer (PT); Health Coach – Advanced Health & Fitness Specialist; American College of Sports Medicine (ACSM) certified – Health Fitness Specialist (HFS); ACSM/National Center on Health, Physical Activity, and Disability (NCHPAD) Certified Inclusive Fitness Trainer (CIFT).

Professional affiliations include: the National Strength and Conditioning Association and International Society of Sports Biomechanics.

Jones is a member of the Executive Women's Golf Association (EWGA) and a sponsor of the EWGA Chicago Metro chapter. Her website is: www.jacque-jonesfitness.com.

CHAPTER 14

A Career Game for Position, Power and Profit

By Joan C. Cavanaugh

Over the course of three careers, nothing has influenced my life as much as my "fourth career" in the game of golf. At age 9, I was introduced to golf indirectly because my older brother, Don, caddied on the weekends for our rich uncle at Beverly Country Club on the south side of Chicago. I thought golf was about making money because he always arrived home with tips and one year, he even paid for my high school uniform and my tuition.

I never thought about it again until 40 years later when a good friend told me that he was a golfer. I remember saying, "Oh that's wonderful," or something like that, and he said, "I don't think you understand. It means I play golf after work and on all weekends." And I responded, "That's fine, because I need to work on my new publishing business 24/7."

Little did I know that my response was a prerequisite to a marriage proposal less than a month later. Within nine months, I was engaged in Venice, Italy and honeymooned in Palm Springs, Calif. It seemed that golf might be playing an important part in my life even then. I had no idea that this game would eventually lead to a career.

It did not happen right away. In fact, it was a year later that my husband Joe finally got me to his country club one Sunday morning with an invitation for breakfast and an introduction to a golf club – meaning, the club you hit a ball with. I resisted previous invitations with valid arguments, such as, "I don't have time to play," or "a round of golf is too expensive for a four-hour game." In addition to that, I am not athletic.

But I did go with him that Sunday and after breakfast, he escorted me to the golf range, put a club in my hands and showed me how to swing it. Less than 20 minutes later, an announcement blared over the P.A. system that Mr. and Mrs. Cavanaugh-Chickvary would be the next couple on the tee. Could it be that I was about to experience the real thing, actually playing golf?

If I refused, I risked disappointing Joe, my best friend, my confidant, my love, and my husband. Overcome with fear and embarrassment, but with prayerful resolve, I followed him to the first tee where the Sunday morning men's club was lined up in their carts ready to watch just how Joe's wife hit the ball. No one there knew this was my first swing ever.

Thoughts like this rose up in the heat of the moment. How could I, as a successful entrepreneur, experienced middle-aged business women, winner of business awards, radio and TV guest, hope to hit this very small ball out there on that expanse of green grass and not experience fear and failure?

At that moment, my years of self-esteem failed me. Joe teed up the ball and I swung the club. The little white ball careened high and far before landing out on the fairway. I was shocked at the results and Joe said the magic words: "You have a natural swing." And at that moment, with a full chest, I surrendered to the game and have never looked back.

A while later, I responded to an invitation to join an Executive Women's Golf Association in my local community. Cautiously, I accepted the invitation to an introductory tee-off dinner just to see how good these women golfers were. I didn't know how good one had to be to play business golf.

What I really liked about this EWGA group was the fun I had with them that night. The laughter abounded at our table and all around the room of 200 women. I decided if this is what business golf was all about, I'm in! I was also sure that in the company of such women, I could learn more about this game.

I realized it was up to me to use this network as effectively as possible and to definitely promote my new business. I researched issues about women and business golf, but I was puzzled. Why were women not considering business golf for success like the men who played golf for power, positions and profit?

The research documented that women are better educated, have more academic degrees, are greater consumers and outnumber men as entrepreneurs, but that we still lack parity in the workforce. I was aware that women are not always invited to private "men caves" for informal meetings away from the office, where deals are made and bonding relationships are forged. If the golf course is an informal meeting place away from the office, I wondered if women were missing the point?

Golf has often been the traditional path to advancement in a man's career – a place where he is visible to his boss and because of that, he can parlay for advancement, discuss company trends, entertain clients and create strategic relationships, which could foster big deals. I decided that the game of golf is an opportunity to invest in success, not only in business, but also in life. It is available to women – and to me.

In the time I spent building my business, I discovered this to be true. Because I played the game, I found the right reps for my publishing activities, creative designers for my products and catalogues, leads to new distribution areas and the ongoing development of strategic relationships with colleagues that led to new ideas, new markets, publicity and introductions.

While honing my golf skills, I found ways to share my love and understanding of the value of the game by founding LPGA-USGA Girls Golf programs in several states. I successfully sold my publishing company and in 2010, I founded

Boardroom Golf. My mission was to empower women on how to use business golf as a tool to advance their careers. I would engage women business associations in major cities with keynote presentations and interactive workshops about women and business golf.

I was elected to the presidency of the EWGA Connecticut chapter and then received an invitation to serve on the EWGA's national board. I helped establish the EWGA Foundation and became one of its first presidents. My college alumni magazine wrote about me, citing not only my leadership in golf, but also my accomplishments in museum education and the development of my new publishing company.

The ministry of Thailand sought the curriculum expertise of the college's International Outreach Center, promoting cultural and educational exchanges between Southeast and East Asia. The article about me landed on the desk of one of the officers of the ministry and I consequently received an invitation from his office to give a business workshop in Bangkok to 150 university professors and museum educators.

Shortly after accepting the invitation, I received a call from Thailand's Office of the Ministry asking me to bring my golf clubs. I knew Thailand was a long trip and that I would need to bring luggage and workshop materials too, so I declined. The next day, I received a second call with the query about the brand of golf clubs that I used. The caller promised that the clubs of my choice would be awaiting me on my arrival. Then it dawned on me that I might have received this workshop invitation because I golf.

Imagine flying first class on Thai Airlines, being picked up by a limousine and greeted by my own translator just to play a game of golf! I sent an email to all my golf colleagues that I was to play one of the finest private golf courses in Thailand with an elected magistrate of the Thai government. I am convinced that week in Bangkok was more of an invitation to play golf than for the successful educational workshop I presented.

I thought of a quotation by Bob Hope that I saw a few years ago at the World Golf Hall of Fame Museum in St. Augustine, Fla. Hope said: "I never dreamed when I took up golf that someday, I'd be playing with kings and presidents, actors and singers, television stars and generals, corporate tycoons, athletes and club owners. Golf is a bond that has drawn us all together and created a special fraternity among the celebrities of show business, sports and politics."

Golf gives a woman visibility. I occasionally arrive at a New York networking event with my two-club Ping golf bag over my shoulder. It helps me make the point that if you want visibility in the workplace for position, power and profit, you need to join the legions of business golfers. I then relay countless stories about those who stop me on the street to inquire, "Where do you play? Is that an Odyssey White Hot putter?"

I was once tapped on the shoulder by a guy in an elevator who asked, "Aren't you the golfing lady?" Yes, just as I thought when I was 9, golf is about making money, but it is so much more than that. It's about acceptance in the business world into a community of intelligent, fun-loving companions who believe as Plato did, who wrote centuries ago. "You can discover more about a person in an hour of play than a year of conversation."

I never thought that I was athletic, but now I am part of a sporting community because I have come to understand that golf is a mental game. Golf, itself, has the built-in formula of game strategy for me to practice the principles of good business savvy, preparing a pre-game plan, focusing on a target, accessing hazardous situations, making strategic decisions, sizing-up clients, practicing team play, using clever tension-breaking quips, realizing attainable goals, meeting challenges and leading. For golf, it's one shot at a time; for business, it's one move at a time. Golf is a career game, for sure.

In speaking engagements at universities, women's organizations, conferences and corporations, both here and abroad, I try to offer tips on how to forge career success through business golf. I want women to realize that like anything else in life that's worth doing, you don't wait to be invited. You must step up and take charge.

Isn't that our unique forte as women? So, when the head golf pro announces your name over the loud speaker, pick yourself up, walk to the first tee and a whole new world of challenges await you.

About Joan C. Cavanaugh

Joan C. Cavanaugh is the founder and CEO of Boardroom Golf. Boardroom Golf's mission is to empower a woman to use golf to further her career and eventually reach a place in the boardroom. As a certified business golf expert with 25 years of playing business golf, she coaches businesswomen, showing how to maximize the social networking skills of the golf game. Since business golf is a means to building strategic relationships, it becomes a tool for building a successful career.

Joan is a speaker and master teacher, and she simplifies the game for new golfers, as well as for experienced golfers who need relationship skills to be effective. Through one-to-one coaching sessions, interactive workshops and in-house corporate forums, she provides step-by-step skill building designed to develop rapport with power brokers and decision makers. She also demonstrates how leadership and business savvy practiced on the golf course work to enhance a business career.

Joan received the EWGA's 2003 Canon USA Businesswoman of the Year Award and the 2004 Office Depot Businesswoman of the Year Award. She has been a master teacher in academia, a corporate administrator for the Metropolitan Museum of Art and the founder and CEO of an international publishing company. She served on the national board of the Executive Women's Golf Association, a women's committee for the USGA and was the founder and site director of several LPGA-USGA Girls Golf programs. She is a member of the EWGA, USGA and Women in the Golf Industry, Manhattan Chamber of Commerce, TLC, APW and NAWBO.

CHAPTER 15

From LPGA Career to TV Broadcast Booth, Golf Has Been A Blessing

By Judy Rankin

It's hard to believe I have been in television for 30 years. In fact, some people forget that I ever played on the LPGA Tour. But my playing experience prepared me for television and at a crisis time in my golf life, television kept me in the golf industry. In retrospect, my bad back probably turned out to be a blessing.

I got started in the game at 6 years old. My father played public course golf and was a Ben Hogan fan. I learned through a trial and error method and my game always reflected some of that teaching. When I was a little girl, our family life took a very serious turn when my mother became terminally ill. We lost her when I was 11.

I had a great deal of success as a child, and later on as a junior player. Pursuing competitive golf as a career was not very realistic at that time. There were not many professional players and even less money. The idea was to play a very high level of amateur golf. My father convinced me that golf would improve my life and open many doors. As my story played out he was certainly right.

A lot of good and some bad happened along the way and, at 17, I found myself on the LPGA Tour. It was so very different than it is today for the teenagers that play the tour. I can't even draw a comparison. Do I believe I was too young? Yes, given everything I know today. I found the whole experience very daunting. I believe it delayed my success as a player, but I can't discount experiences, friendships, and the things I learned along the way.

A big influence was PGA pro and golf instructor, Bob Toski. I began working for him at Ocean Reef Golf Club in Key Largo, Fla., in the winter months the year I turned 19. He gave me a broader understanding of the game and it was with my father's blessing.

The next real influence on my life and game was my husband, Yippy Rankin. My golf skill and his football competitive mentality seemed to mesh together and make me a little tougher at a time when I needed it. I met Yippy at a tournament in Midland, Texas when he played in a pro-am with Marlene Hagge. I was 21 when we got married in 1967. Even though I was successful, I didn't become a winner until after our son was born. Family life was good for me and what I always believed I wanted. We all pursued my career and the rest is history.

Serious back problems changed my game and my world, for that matter. My health and playing poorly drove me away from the LPGA Tour. Little did I know that the next great opportunity would come along in the name of ABC Sports. I had always loved television golf but didn't believe it would be for me because of my fear of speaking in public. Surprise! I accepted an offer in 1984 to do what Bob "Rossie" Rosburg did on the fairways at the U.S. Women's Open. The role was small at that time. Even though I was intimidated, I pulled it off.

The next career changing event was being asked to work at the 1985 U.S. (men's) Open at Oakland Hills, in Michigan. New nerves emerged and I have to thank so many people, mainly men, that I worked with who helped me, encouraged me, and made me believe I could do this. Over time I was fortunate to work with people like Jim McKay, Jack Whittaker, Brent Musburger,

Terry Gannon, Mike Tirico, and many other talented people. I also worked with numerous golf professionals, such as Curtis Strange, Paul Azinger, Nick Faldo, Jack Nicklaus, Andy North, and the very unique Peter Alliss. They were all a huge part of my education. It does take an entire team in front of the camera and behind the scenes to put golf on the air. My one amazement, and still today, is that your screen never goes black! Perhaps the best advice I ever received and maybe the reason I made it in this man's world was this, "We don't want your expertise as a woman, we want your expertise as a golfer." My producers at ABC Sports made it clear that the telecasts were not about us, the commentators. It was about the golf, the players, the golf course, and the championship.

This current part of my career has been the greatest ride. I don't feel like I'm on a career ladder. I don't feel like I have to beat anybody out. I remain grateful to ESPN and the Golf Channel, more than thirty years later, that I'm still employed. Television has allowed me to have a little more fun. I'm not on the practice tee every day. If I make a mistake, I can edit myself. Ironically, I became more recognized because of TV and working in men's golf than I ever experienced as a player.

Looking back, I realize that a lot of people made an investment in my career years ago. My family has been in this boat with me all along and they've shared in my successes. If raising a child takes a village, then raising a tour player takes everybody in your life. When I was inducted into the World Golf Hall of Fame, it meant a lot not just to me, but also to my family. Many people play a large role for anybody who gets into the Hall of Fame.

Right along with the people I love and the home I've made, golf has been my life. And in Part II to my career in golf, one thing I've learned is that within reason, your ability to do something is directly related to your desire to do it. I'm older, but I'm wiser and I'm more relaxed. I was never a great athlete or a great physical specimen, but golf found me. And golf in my life has certainly been a great blessing.

About Judy Rankin

A St. Louis native, Judy Torluemke Rankin joined the LPGA Tour in 1962 at age 17. She played professionally and won 26 LPGA tournaments until back problems ended her career in 1983.

During her LPGA career, she led the tour's season money list and was the LPGA's Player of the Year in 1976 and 1977. She won the tour's Vare Trophy for low scoring average three times – in 1973, 1976, and 1977. Rankin won six tournaments in 1976 and set a single-season earnings record of $150,734, becoming the first LPGA player to cross $100,000 in a season.

While she never won a major championship, two of the tournaments she won – the Colgate Dinah Shore, which became the Kraft Nabisco Championship, and the Peter Jackson Classic, which became du Maurier Classic, a former major – were later elevated to major championship status on the LPGA Tour.

Rankin served as captain of two winning U.S. Solheim Cup teams (1996 and 1998) and was inducted into the World Golf Hall of Fame in 2000. She was presented the Bob Jones Award in 2002 for distinguished sportsmanship in golf. Rankin was honored on the St. Louis Walk of Fame in 2013.

Following her playing career, she became a golf commentator for ESPN/ABC-Sports and the Golf Channel, offering television commentary for both men's and women's professional events.

Rankin is a breast-cancer survivor. She was married to Yippy Rankin for 45 years, who passed away in 2012. Her son, Tuey Rankin, was one of the first children to travel on the LPGA Tour.

CHAPTER 16

Business Golf Puts You on Par for Success

By Karen Furtado

When I first took up the game of golf, I did so for several reasons.

First, I needed a different sport to play. Softball was fun, but I needed to find a sport where I no longer suffered continuous injuries and one that would afford the opportunity to reap professional benefits. Secondly, as a result of growing up in a family with six brothers where we competed daily, I needed to find a way to channel my competitive energy.

The third reason I took up golf was simply a business decision. More and more, I realized I was being excluded from key business events because I did not know how to play the game. I could see the value of being part of the golf experience and I wanted "in!" Fortunately, there was an EWGA chapter just beginning in my new community and I took full advantage of their offerings to learn the fundamentals of golf.

Previously, I had struggled with the notion that golf was only a sport and therefore believed it did not belong in the business world. Now, armed with the necessary skills of my new sport, I needed to learn how to apply it to the work environment. If you have ever struggled with that same mindset regarding the role of golf in the business world, my stories may provide you with some helpful insight into how golf and work can be perfect companions.

I have spent my entire professional career in the insurance industry where traditionally, the majority of the executives are men. When I rose to the rank of vice president in a large, global firm, I came to realize how golf is often an equalizer in professional relationships and serves as an invaluable business tool for those who can master the art of *business golf*.

Business golf is one of the most effective professional tools anyone can bring to the office. Business truly does take place on the golf course. Golf can be about building lasting and meaningful relationships; that common connection, the priceless trust in a colleague or a client that will serve everyone involved. There are times when you will use these golf-created and nurtured relationships to move a deal along or even close a deal.

I learned early in my career how valuable business golf relationships can be. I can recall two nearly impossible situations in my work life had I not worked to develop a deeper, more significant relationship with my clients.

The first lesson involved an insurance company for whom we processed a significant component of their business. This was a business partnership that had lasted many years. As a new vice president, I carried with me the strong, positive relationship I had nurtured with the CEO.

However, working with the CIO had always proven to be a challenge. I contemplated how to make a difference with this individual. I decided to invite the CEO for a golf outing, hoping he may have the insights I needed to meet the goal of improving my relationship with the CIO. We played a wonderful round of golf and headed into the clubhouse for what became a significant conversation. Not only did I acquire the necessary insights to deal with the CIO, I gained a professional mentor. To this day, more than 15 years later, he continues to graciously share valuable thoughts and perceptions on all aspects of business with me.

The second lesson came many years later while I was the lead executive for the acquisition of a company in the process of bankruptcy. A year after the procurement, I discovered the new management team of their largest client wanted to head in a different direction; they were more of a hands-on team and did not want another firm performing the services for them. This was going to be a challenge.

We had another five years on the contract and if you have ever been in this situation, you know that if a client does not really want to use certain services, they will never be satisfied. The only option they considered was to take the services back. The challenge is to be certain you are solving the right problem. Did they really want to "take back" their services or was there a way to satisfy their needs until the contract expired? Obviously, a face-to-face meeting was in order.

As we discussed the details of the meeting, we opted to spend the day on the golf course at LaCosta in Carlsbad, Calif. I learned many things about the customer that day. I learned about his industry experience, his philosophies on business, what his drivers were and more – all while playing a round of golf.

Following the round, we outlined the agreement, which would end the contract early, but leave both companies whole. It took two more rounds of golf to work out the details, resulting in a real win/win agreement. I can say with great certainty, it would never have been possible if we had not built a close relationship in a short period of time. The lessons I learned from the first day of playing golf with the executive were invaluable to developing the kind of relationship needed to work through the details of the business arrangement.

You can gain valuable insight into someone's business ethics by observing the way they handle themselves on the golf course. Do they observe the rules and regulations of golf? Do they follow them only when someone is watching? Do they practice the time-honored etiquette of the game? Do they live in their own world on the course or are they supportive of the entire group?

From my experiences, I can tell you that these translate into guiding principles in business. Imagine having an employee or a colleague who is always trying to cut corners and not following the rules or specific regulations for an industry, in an effort to "get away with it." These things do happen – and unfortunately, they happen every day.

The majority of my encounters involving business golf have been with individuals who respect and follow the rules of the game. However, there are always those who make you realize this is not true of everyone. Let me illustrate the point with an example.

I often play golf when I attend conferences around the country. Once, in Tucson, Ariz., I arrived a day early so I could go out and enjoy a round of golf before the big events began. I was paired with three other conference attendees. We arrived at this very short 275-yard, par-4 hole. My tee shot had landed just short of the green on the left side.

As we arrived at the green, I saw my ball, nestled right next to a rock. Ugh – what do I do now? The only option, other than taking an unplayable lie, was to chip it out backwards to set up my third shot. My playing partners stopped me to ask what I was doing. They suggested I nudge it out from the rock and hit my second shot. We discussed the options and it was clear to me that they never considered following the rules of the game and playing the ball as it lies.

I realized that for these three individuals, when faced with an obstacle that had an easy, but unethical solution - which would most likely not be discovered - it appeared as if they would make that choice in a heartbeat. My level of trust with these three, which was high on the first tee, immediately changed as a result of this experience. Your actions on the golf course speak loudly about your personal and professional character and unfortunately, are transferable to the workplace.

One of the most challenging lessons to learn about business golf is that at the end of the day, it is as much about business as it is about golf. It is not about improving your handicap or scoring the lowest round in the foursome. It is about building relationships in the most positive and sustainable manner possible. I know not everyone believes in this philosophy.

I will tell you that it is difficult to stand at the forward tees and already know you are going to smoke your drive several yards past the president of the company that you are trying to work with on an important business deal. I have always felt there are two options – take a different club or head back to the white tees. There is a balance to be found in being competitive and building relationships. Keep in mind that during these times on a golf course, it is about business, and if you stay focused on your goal, it will pay dividends over and over!

I have learned over the years that course management is the key to a lower score. Hitting the ball as far as I possibly can does not always yield the best result. As a matter of fact, there have been countless times where I will play a club for what its maximum yardage could be. For example, I can typically hit my 7-iron about 135 yards, but occasionally, it will travel 140 to 145 yards. That may only happen about five percent of the time, but 100 percent of the time, I play like my ball will go that far.

There is a balance between taking a risk using the information you have available and just "going for it" every time, hoping for a different outcome. Work to find it. Golf, as in business, always requires you to consider all the necessary information and adjust your game plan accordingly. To achieve this balance and acquire these skills, just as in golf, you need to practice. Put in the time and effort and the outcome will be rewarding.

Time on the links, in the cart, and sitting in the clubhouse, are all opportunities to develop deeper relationships with clients and colleagues that will sustain you through the successes and challenges during your professional career. They will present opportunities for you to solve business problems, deepen a relationship or close a deal.

Learn the game, obey the rules, follow the proper etiquette, make the connections, honor the relationships, and most of all, enjoy the results!

About Karen Furtado

Karen Furtado, is currently the chair of the LPGA Foundation Board of Directors. She has served as President of the Executive Women's Golf Association Board of Directors from 2008 - 2009. Ms. Furtado is a true testament to the organization's success in attracting women into the sport. A 21-year member of the 22-year old EWGA, Karen has experienced first-hand the benefits of organized play activities, championship competition, networking and game improvement programs. As a member of the Southern New Hampshire Chapter, she was a chapter board member, then moving into a regional director volunteer role in New England before joining the EWGA Board of Directors. She has served as President of the EWGA Foundation Board of Directors as well.

Her proficiency with the game of golf complements her successful professional career track, which involves more than 25 years of business and technical experience within the insurance industry. Karen is a Partner at Strategy Meets Action, a leading strategic advisory firm servicing both insurance companies and solution providers. She has exceptional knowledge of policy administration, rating, product configuration, billing, and claims and deep understanding of distribution and emerging technologies such as social media, cloud/SaaS, and ideation/crowdsourcing. She also knows how to modernize and innovate for competitive advantage.

Karen has held various leadership positions, including insurance practice director at Collaborative Consulting and vice president of CGI's Insurance Practice.

Karen is often quoted in major insurance publications and speaks frequently at leading industry conferences. She holds a Bachelor of Science degree in Rehabilitation Counseling & Physical Therapy from Springfield College.

CHAPTER 17

Golf: My Inner Path to Happiness

By Karen Palacios-Jansen

Golf and fitness have been important to me for most of my life and I will be forever grateful to my parents for introducing me to the game and encouraging me to follow my passion.

Golf has allowed me to develop a unique career and lifestyle. It has taught me work ethic and incredible life lessons. It has allowed me to meet the most amazing people and has given me many opportunities to see the world that I may not have otherwise known.

It's sometimes said that "golf is a metaphor for life" – the idea being that the highs and lows we experience on the golf course teach us how to face similar challenges we experience in everyday life. We can't always hit the perfect shot, but we can learn from our bad shots as we can learn from our failures in life.

For many of us who play golf, it becomes a teaching tool for us to overcome our fears and faults. To illustrate that, I would like to share with you parts of my golf story that I have not shared with many people. It's about how I overcame depression and low self-esteem as a young woman and with the help of therapy, exercise, family support and, of course, golf, developed into a confident and happy person.

After a painful divorce in my early 20s, I suffered bouts of deep depression. It was not the kind that made me incapable of functioning on a day-to-day basis, but my depression ate away at me, leaving only a small part of the person I used to be growing up as a carefree kid.

I grew up playing golf. I had one of those storybook childhoods where I grew up living on a golf course. I played golf, swam or took tennis lessons. I got good enough in golf to play on an NCAA Division I university team.

After college, I immediately got married and started living what seemed like a perfect life. I married a man eight years older who was not only a dentist, but was back at school studying to become a medical doctor.

I had married the man of my dreams, but unfortunately, my husband had not married the woman of his dreams. He met another woman a couple of years after we were married while he was at medical school and he announced one day that they were having a baby. Nothing could have prepared me to cope with or understand that kind of rejection. I was now 24 years old and divorced.

My parents, who would have been happy for me to return home and live with them, knew that would not help my situation. Reluctantly, they encouraged me to move away and seek a new life, even if it meant moving several thousand miles away to another state. Looking back, making this move changed the course of my life to help me create not only a unique career in golf, but to also find new love.

While I was in college, I took lessons from – at the time – an unknown teaching pro named David Leadbetter. By the time I graduated from college, had been married for a few years and divorced six years later, David Leadbetter had become the world's most renowned golf teacher coaching the likes of Nick Faldo, Nick Price and Payne Stewart.

After my divorce, I moved to Orlando, Fla., to play golf tournaments and eventually ended up taking lessons from Mr. Leadbetter and his assistants at the David Leadbetter Golf Academy at Lake Nona Country Club. I spent so much time there taking lessons and practicing that they asked me to help assist with the golf schools. Eventually, I became a golf teacher.

I somehow found my niche in life and that was teaching, talking and writing about golf. Through Mr. Leadbetter, I met and spent time with some of the world's best golfers, including Ernie Els, Seve Ballesteros, Trevor Immelman and Se Ri Pak.

And because I spoke fluent Spanish, I traveled all over South America representing the David Leadbetter Golf Academy, teaching golf and coaching junior players. I was even dating one of the other up-and-coming golf teachers. All seemed to be well.

I was also appearing as a guest golf instructor on a new cable channel called the Golf Channel. I even made the cover of *Golf for Women Magazine* twice, being touted as one of the best young female teaching pros. But what I wasn't doing was dealing with my emotions. Feelings of rejection and unworthiness still haunted me from my divorce.

I would suppress those feelings. For weeks, I would go to work and do all the right things there, and then go home and be by myself, crying, not sleeping or eating. I didn't know what was wrong with me, or why I couldn't just be happy like everyone else.

One of the things I did to feel better was to exercise. The process of working out made me feel temporarily happy. You see, when you exercise, your brain releases certain chemicals that work together to make you feel good. Exercise also raises your body temperature, which produces a calming effect. After exercising, I felt a sense of accomplishment.

Once I recognized this, I started taking every kind of exercise class I could find. I would play golf every day, go waterskiing, jogging, rollerblading – anything I could physically do to help boost my mood. Playing golf with clients or friends and working out were my happiest times.

Although I had a boyfriend, a great job and plenty of friends and family support, I still felt sadness. I was getting close to 30, was not married and without children. Many of my friends were now starting families.

I had always wanted that for myself, but the years were flying by and it didn't seem like that would ever happen for me. Feelings of insecurity overwhelmed me. I thought there must be something wrong with me.

Although depression seemed to overtake my life, golf and exercise were the two constants that helped me push through the hard times. And, you can't play golf when you are crying!

I could be depressed, but at the same time look forward to playing a tournament on a new golf course. I was at my calmest when I was walking down the fairway anticipating my next shot. Exercise had the same effect and years later, I would combine these two disciplines into a unique golf fitness program called Cardiogolf.

Working at a world-famous golf academy, we would get the occasional celebrity sightings, including those of Michael Douglas, Catherine Zeta-Jones, Sylvester Stallone and Michael Bolton. Scheduled for lessons one day was Dan Jansen, the reigning Olympic gold medalist in speed skating, the world record holder for the 1,000 meters and an inspiration to millions who watched him overcome tremendous obstacles during his career.

I got to spend time with Dan over the next few days assisting with his lessons with David Leadbetter and taking him on the golf course. At the end of the weekend, we took a picture together and he signed it for me: "Thanks for the great lessons." I would not see Dan again until four years later.

Five years later, I was still working for David Leadbetter and dating the same guy. Although a kind person, my boyfriend didn't want to get married. He had problems of his own, including abandonment issues and he could never fully commit to himself, let alone to me. Why didn't my boyfriend want to marry me?

It was not until I moved to Miami a few years later, that I finally sought professional help for my depression. Through therapy, I discovered that marriage did not validate me as a woman or as a good person. I was always loved and valued and good enough exactly the way I was.

I finally came out of my funk a year later. I moved into a new apartment in Miami's South Beach. Working long hours, I didn't have time to unpack boxes, so my cleaning lady took it upon herself to decorate my apartment for me. She unpacked my pictures and put the framed picture of Dan Jansen on the wall right by the front door.

Every day I left my house in the morning, I'd look at the picture and say, "See you later, Dan Jansen, have a great day," and then when I would come home in the afternoon after work, I would say to the picture, "Did you have a good day? What have you been doing all day, Dan Jansen?"

This was in September 1999. In March 2000, I re-met Dan four years after our first encounter. We both had been invited to play in a Gary Player charity golf event. At breakfast, Dan tapped me on the shoulder and said to me, "Karen, I am Dan Jansen. You gave me some lessons four years ago. Do you remember me?"

I like golf because it combines the merits of a great sport, offers exercise and the chance to be in a beautiful environment, and provides the excitement of competition and challenge. It also offers the chance to meet and get to know wonderful people.

Dan and I were married 10 months later and I have never been happier in my life. If you are depressed, you may unknowingly make yourself unavailable for friendship and love. Looking back, I have wondered why Dan and I didn't get together the first time we met.

Depression can distort your thinking and create negativity. It's very hard to think of others when all you can think of is your own pain. I couldn't see how someone like Dan Jansen could be interested in someone like me. In time, I was finally able to recognize that I was a good person, married or not. I finally was in a place that I could meet someone and get married again.

My advice to anyone who has ever experienced depression is to seek professional care. Take action and find a solution. When you talk to others, you will realize that it can happen to anyone and that there are solutions. Research shows that finding joy in daily tasks or in a hobby can help overcome depression. For me, playing golf and exercising were the two things that I could immerse myself in and be happy. I hope these two things can help you find your happiness, as well.

About Karen Palacios-Jansen:

LPGA teaching professional Karen Palacios- Jansen, 2008 LPGA National Teacher of the Year, has been voted one of America's "Top 50 Best Women Teachers" by Golf Digest Magazine since 1998. Jansen has her own golf events company, Swing Blade Enterprises, in Mooresville, N.C. She served for several years as managing editor for Golf Fitness Magazine.

Jansen is a Nike Golf Performance Specialist, as well as an AFAA Certified Personal Trainer. She developed a unique golf-specific fitness system called Cardiogolf.

Jansen is also a member of The Nike Golf Advisory Staff, for which she participates in Nike product development and promotions.

A former David Leadbetter-trained instructor and Jim McLean Golf School master instructor, Jansen has taught golf for 19 years and has appeared numerous times as a guest instructor on the The Golf Channel. Jansen is also the author of the Golf Fitness, a book dedicated to physical and mental conditioning for golf.

Jansen is married to Olympic gold medalist speed skater Dan Jansen. Frequently requested as a public speaker and lecturer at local and national golf shows and conferences, she has helped thousands of golfers improve their golf games. For more information visit www.kpjgolf.com.

CHAPTER 18

Using Golf As A Tool To Work Hard, Play Hard and to Benefit Others

By Kathy Kolder

I never thought about golf in the early part of my career, then one day, John Fry, my business partner, said to me, "You know, you'd better learn how to play golf because one day, we're going to host a PGA Tour tournament. We're going to have the best tournament in the world and it's probably time that you take up the game."

That suggestion came out of the blue, but I agreed, and I started on an amazing path in the game of golf. As a result, golf turned out to be a wonderful business tool. It became a way for me to get out there and spend quality time with a lot of key executives.

Our company even built our own championship 8,053-yard golf course named The Institute. We named it that for our main charity, The American Institute of Mathematics. It proved to be a rare advantage in business. So many of our business partners wanted to play there – many of them executives with whom we couldn't otherwise get a meeting. I'm very lucky that I get to play golf for business quite often.

Of course, there have been many years of hard work and long hours getting to this point. Our company, Fry's Electronics, is now more than 25-years-old with 34 stores in nine states, selling more than 100,000 electronics items, and also servicing our customers with Frys.Com on the Internet.

In addition, since 2006, we also sponsor the PGA Tour's Fry's.com Open each year. We're very proud that our tournament will lead the PGA's Fed Ex Cup season, starting in 2013-2014.

My association with the Fry family started back in 1985, when I was selling computers to John Fry at his father's grocery store chain, Fry's Food Stores. At that time, the only way you could buy a computer was to make an appointment between 9 a.m. and 5 p.m., Monday through Friday, at stores like Businessland or Computerland. John and I thought, "Geez, nobody wants to shop like this. Maybe we should start something different."

So, we figured we could open a grocery-store-type of computer store where customers would have shopping carts, snack foods and all the high-tech gear you would ever want. We would have the little tiny computer chips all the way up to computers. We also would have software, accessories, televisions and stereo equipment.

Of course, as electronics grew, so did our store. We were open on weekends and customers no longer needed an appointment to buy a computer. They could just walk into the store and get what they wanted. Later, we added appliances, music and movies.

Originally, we imagined when we got to five stores, we would just sell it and go off and do something else, which is very common with Silicon Valley companies. But when we got our first offer to sell the company, we said, "Nope, we're still having too much fun. Let's keep going. Let's allow this thing to become as big and as great as we can get it."

I thought I would retire five years after we started the company, and then I said it would be 10 years. Now, I think I'll retire when we stop having fun. We keep growing and adding so many more fun things that retirement is not even in the picture yet.

Time has gone by quickly with our great growth. We now have over 10,000 employees. Originally, I was just looking for a job in sales with an expense account. I never thought I would become a co-founder of a big company. Sometimes, I want to pinch myself and ask, "Is this real?" But most of the time, I'm so busy and I know I just have to keep going, taking it day by day.

I have a favorite quote that says: "Think success again and again, until there is no room in your mind for any doubt. Act boldly on your positive thoughts, and be the success you envision." The reason I like that quote so much is that "success breeds success." If you keep working in small steps and small successes, it will finally lead you to a big success.

It also brings me to another truth, that luck is based on a lot of hard work. Luck just doesn't appear out of nowhere unless you win the lottery. Most of us go through the path of doing a lot of work. You soon realize that's how it works and you stay on that path until you get to where you want to go. It's a wonderful journey.

As a leader of our company, I'm confrontational. That's usually not what people want to hear, but I think it helps make you successful. You can be a great communicator and you can be a really great speaker, but unless you are willing to ask the hard questions and address the hard issues along the path, you're not really going to make it to that top level of success. You have to be ready for "Plan C." Most people have a "Plan A" and a lot of people have a "Plan B," but a "Plan C" covers your worst-case analysis. If you can cover that, then you know you'll be successful.

I try to teach all of our rising leaders that they can't get where they are going if they don't know *where* they are trying to go. If you don't know what path you are trying to follow, you'll never get to the end of it. It's really a focus on what you need to do in order to be successful.

When I started using golf as a tool in our business, I didn't realize how valuable it could be. When you take people out to great courses and you play golf, you get five hours of undivided attention from high-level executives that you'd never get in the office. Plus, you're spending time with them in a beautiful surrounding. It's there on the golf course that you have the ability to really cover key issues in a truly positive focus, to present your story to them, and to get them to buy off on it – maybe even give you help that they might not offer over a desk. It's an amazing tool!

Golf also gives you a way to use it as an analogy in business. When you make a good shot or get out of a bunker, it gives you lots of ways to talk about what's going on in your business and interact with the people with whom you are playing golf.

For example, maybe we are having retail issues, such as how to get allocated product, how to be first to market, or figuring out how we can better manage inventory, and we are out on the golf course with vendors. Golf becomes a great tool to open up conversations that sometimes might be tough to start.

I've certainly had some interesting rounds playing corporate golf. I also have learned a lot playing in our pro-am tournament at our PGA events. I was the only woman playing in the pro-am of our first Fry's.com event and I had no idea what to expect. When we went to the first tee, I was so nervous I could barely hold my clubs. The starter was an older gentleman and he walked over to me and put his arm around my shoulders and said, "You're shaking like a leaf. Don't do that on TV." Fortunately, when it was my turn to hit my tee shot, I hit a great drive.

After my shot, I handed my driver to the person I thought was my caddie. Then suddenly I heard an unusual hush in the crowd, and I knew something went terribly wrong. I thought, "What did I do? Did I split my pants?" I turned around and saw PGA pro, Jason Gore, holding my driver over his head, saying to the gallery, "She thinks I don't even have my tour card! She thinks I'm her caddie!" I turned bright red and apologized, but he turned what could have been my most embarrassing moment into a really great memory.

At another PGA pro-am at the Phoenix Open, I was playing with my group and we reached the 16th hole, which is notoriously rowdy during the tournament. I didn't expect a crowd to be sitting at that hole on a pro-am day, but when we got there, there were about 8,000 people around the green. I heard a few chants of "Go lady!" I hit my shot but it rolled off the green. When I hit the next shot, it went in! I received more cheering for that putt than anything I've ever done in my life! That was probably my most memorable moment in golf.

Sponsoring a PGA Tour tournament was really the dream of my business partners, John Randy and Dave Fry. They had grown up in the grocery store business of their father, Chuck Fry, and had been out to the Kraft Nabisco Championship, formerly called the Nabisco Dinah Shore, for many years as kids. From that experience, they knew what a great advertising vehicle a tournament could be, and also how much fun it was. They wanted to build our tournament into a world-class event and use it as a way to unite our key vendor partners, while giving back to charities in the community.

Now, our goal is to stage the PGA tournament on the course we built and hopefully, that will happen in a few years. We met with most of the golf clubs and school golf teams in the area, as well as with a lot of the women's golf groups to get them involved in our tournament. It takes more than 1,200 volunteers to run one event.

We also sold tickets to the tournament at our retail stores and we visited local charities and golf clubs and asked them to help us sell tickets. If they sold a certain number of tickets, we would give back a percentage of every ticket sold as a donation to their charity or junior golf program. We have many different charities involved, such as The First Tee, Special Olympics, Ballet San Jose, the American Heart Association, and of course, The American Institute of Mathematics. We've given more than $6 million to charities since our first event.

I love my work and I love that I get the opportunity through my job to help others reach their full potential. I try to show my kids that you can combine work with enjoyment to really get the most out of appreciating life. I think that's what I'm most passionate about – that I have the opportunity to be an example to show people just how to do that.

About Kathy Kolder

Kathy Kolder was born in Chicago, Illinois, and is a resident of San Jose, California. Ms. Kolder earned a B.A. in Economics/Mathematics from the University of California Santa Barbara. Early in her career, she held a sales position with a computer/software firm in the San Francisco Bay Area. In 1985, she co-founded Fry's Electronics. She is Executive Vice President of Fry's, and oversees the legal, human resources, risk management, loss prevention, and community relations departments of the company. Ms. Kolder is the Secretary of the Board of Directors of Ballet San Jose, and was the 2013 Chairperson for the Frys.com Open PGA Tour golf tournament.

Fry's Electronics

Based in San Jose, Calif., Fry's was founded as a Silicon Valley retail electronics store to provide a one-stop-shopping environment for the high-tech professional. Fry's continues to keep high-tech professionals supplied with products representing the latest technological trends and advances in the personal computer marketplace. Fry's retails over 50,000 electronics items within each store, now totaling 34. There are currently eight stores in Northern California, nine stores in Southern California, eight stores in Texas, two stores in Arizona and Georgia, and one store each in Oregon, Nevada, Washington, Illinois, and Indiana. Fry's stores range in size from 50,000 to over 180,000 square feet. Fry's customers can also shop with confidence online at www.Frys.com.

CHAPTER 19

Building Relationships and Enriching Lives With Golf

By Kathy O'Neal

Confucius said, "Choose a job you love and you will never have to work a day in your life."

My love affair with ClubCorp and the private club industry began more than 25 years ago when I started my career right out of graduate school. Being part of a company whose mission is to "Build Relationships and Enrich Lives" has given me the opportunity to connect ClubCorp and its members with incredible charities, such as The First Tee and President George W. Bush's Warrior Open.

ClubCorp's involvement with these charities has not only benefitted those they serve, but has also provided members from its clubs nationwide a chance to get involved.

I came from a large family of eight children in Corpus Christi, Texas. My father was an avid golfer and a vocational education teacher at the local high school and junior college. While he would have loved a membership in a private country club, the education of his children took precedence. He was content to take his clubs and a shag bag each afternoon down to the hay field next to our home and hit golf balls. Dad passed away more than 15 years ago, but my brother still finds golf balls in that field he mows for each year's hay crop!

After completing my MBA, working for a company that owned private country clubs seemed like nirvana. I set my sights on ClubCorp and secured a position at one of their newest acquisitions at the time. I was their first director of marketing at a country club with lodging, April Sound Country Club in Conroe, Texas. I promised my dad that he and my mom would be my first guests and he would be my first and best golf partner at April Sound.

I spent two wonderful years launching this club and was rewarded with a promotion that took me back to ClubCorp's home office in Dallas to work on their latest and most prestigious acquisition – Firestone Country Club in Akron, Ohio. I wore many hats and worked in market research, club development, membership enrollment and member retention (aka, member happiness).

At one point, after seven years with ClubCorp, I was laid off during a major reorganization. I used that time to get involved at an industry level, writing marketing and market research publications for the National Golf Course Owners Association and the National Golf Foundation. Speaking engagements at their national conferences gave me an opportunity to meet representatives and executives from all over the world.

At one such conference presentation, the first country club manager and founder of the Club Managers Association of China invited me to come to China and speak to his club managers about membership and club marketing. I was the first woman ever to address this group. Translators were there to facilitate the presentation. The only word they had problems translating was my Texan "ya'll" that slipped out from time to time! Their conference was in Beijing that year and they have since invited me back to conduct a marketing workshop in Tianjin.

Armed with international experience, I was recruited to return as an employee at ClubCorp when its executives discovered what they were paying me in consulting fees. My current day-to-day role is to establish relationships at a national level with entities that will encourage greater involvement in ClubCorp's clubs by its members. ClubCorp believes that "users are dues-ers" and the more members use the clubs, the greater the value they derive from the dues they pay to belong. Its members are also very philanthropically minded, and getting the clubs involved in supporting major charities throughout the United States through the game they love provides a tremendous sense of pride at the clubs.

One of the relationships developed through my service on the national board of the Executive Women's Golf Association, Sandy Cross of the PGA of America, was updating the board on the military initiative being launched nationwide by the PGA. Realizing that so many of the 300,000-plus members within ClubCorp are veterans or have family members or friends who are, I knew it was a cause they would embrace.

Sandy introduced me to PGA of America Senior Writer Bob Denney, who provided me with contacts at Salute Military Golf of America (SMGA) and Golf for Injured Veterans Everywhere (GIVE). These organizations help veterans get back into life through the game of golf. Golf becomes a therapeutic tool to help those who have suffered a variety of injuries.

With the wholehearted support of ClubCorp's executives, the directors of golf in clubs nationwide hosted a variety of fun and unique fundraisers over Memorial Day weekend in 2011. Members opened their hearts and their pockets and over that one weekend, contributed more than $70,000. That tradition was repeated for the next two years, and more than $200,000 has been given to SMGA, GIVE and Clearview Hope, a golf program for women veterans.

But the story gets even better. Mr. Denney called me one day to say that he had received a call from the office of President George W. Bush in Dallas. The staff member explained that President Bush wished to heighten the awareness of courage and determination of veterans of the wars on terror and he wished to host a "U.S. Open for Wounded Warriors" and was asking the PGA of America for advice.

Denney told them about ClubCorp's efforts for military veterans and suggested that one of the clubs would be appropriate for the president's tournament. ClubCorp was honored to host the inaugural Warrior Open at Las Colinas Country Club in Irving, Texas in October 2011.

President Bush himself asked to host a "town hall meeting" with the members of Las Colinas Country Club to thank them for providing their course and to ask for their assistance as volunteers during the tournament. The President and Mrs. Bush hosted the warriors, their families and some of the sponsors in their home during the tournament.

The members enthusiastically volunteered and cheered for the first 20 severely wounded veterans as they competed in the two-day competition. I witnessed courageous, determined veterans playing the game after losing limbs, losing eyesight or dealing with post-traumatic stress syndrome. As they negotiated the course's hilly North Texas terrain, they also faced challenges with their prostheses.

Las Colinas Country Club members have served as caddies, scorekeepers and general ambassadors for 65 warriors who have since competed in three Warrior Opens hosted at their club by President Bush. Members have expressed gratitude for the chance to meet these veterans and anticipate future Warrior Opens at their club.

Other partners, like The First Tee, have utilized golf to make a difference in the lives of youth. I represent ClubCorp on The First Tee Board of Dallas and work with executives from around the city to raise dollars and encourage volunteers and golf courses to support their efforts.

The First Tee is not just about teaching golf to youth of all backgrounds; it's about teaching them core values, such as honesty, integrity and leadership. Meeting the kids involved and hearing the stories of what golf and The First Tee have meant in their lives is truly inspiring.

ClubCorp supports The First Tee by hosting many of their tournaments and programs on its courses and involves club members as volunteers. Its directors of golf host golf marathons each year – that's 100 holes of golf in one day – to raise dollars for local and national chapters of The First Tee.

Beyond providing relationships and involvement opportunities for ClubCorp clubs and members, one of the greatest challenges is encouraging more individuals – especially women – to take up the game. During her tenure as executive director of Golf 20/20, Cathy Harbin, ClubCorp's vice president of golf, authored "It's Okay to Play Golf for Fun."

This list encourages members to tee up their golf ball in the fairway; throw their golf balls out of the bunker; or to only chip or putt on holes and not keep score – an effort to debunk the game's seriousness for those just getting into golf. ClubCorp clubs nationwide are challenged to fill the club calendar with competitive and fun programming for all ages and levels of golfers.

Using the many opportunities I have to speak to groups across the country or to publish articles in industry magazines, I try to dispel some of the myths around the game of golf. It is no wonder that only 19.3 percent of the 25.7 million golfers in the U.S. are women. What typical multi-tasking woman has time for a five-hour round of golf on Saturday or Sunday?

What about spending quality time with spouses, children and friends? Are there any health benefits – physical or mental – derived from engaging in golf? Most golfers don't realize that playing nine holes (or even three to six holes of golf) with their children after work or school is possible. New programming in the clubs called "Sunday Fun-days" provides quality time for families seeking leisurely bonding activities. For those seeking calorie-burning challenges in a natural environment, walking the course with a pull cart is available at almost all ClubCorp clubs.

Like most golfers, I talk a good game, but am resolute with my relatively high handicap (26 and improving!) I love the looks on the faces of audiences when I quote statistics revealing the average score of male golfers is 97 and 114 for female golfers. I hear murmurs of, "I'm really not such a bad golfer after all." My husband and I enjoy playing nine holes on Saturday and join other couples for another round on Sunday. Our reward for our efforts is usually brunch at the club before or after our round.

Encouragement for participation in the game, and ultimately joining a private club, comes when people realize that golf can provide an array of advantages to participants. Most parents don't realize this safe, non-contact sport is a great way to earn scholarships. Women's college golf scholarships are often available to high school girls who can break 90. The sport is also a great way for couples to spend quality time or for singles to meet other singles with similar interests.

Whether utilizing golf for life-changing therapy, fundraising, teaching life's important lessons to youth or simply helping couples, families and friends enjoy good times together, golf is truly about building relationships and enriching lives. I have been blessed that golf has played such an integral role in my life and career.

About Kathy O'Neal

Kathy O'Neal was born and raised in Corpus Christi, Texas. She earned her bachelor's degree in English from the University of Texas and an MBA from Southern Methodist University in Dallas.

She spent two years as a paralegal working for the chief justice of the Texas Supreme Court. She began with ClubCorp as director of marketing for April Sound Country Club and has served in a variety of roles for the company, including market research, new club development, membership enrollment and membership retention.

She has been named among the "Most Prominent Women in the Club Industry in 2010" by Boardroom Magazine and among the "Most Influential Irish Women of 2010" by Irish Voice Magazine. She has been a frequent speaker at the Club Managers Association of America annual conferences and has written a number of publications for the National Golf Course Owners Association on marketing and market research for golf clubs.

Kathy currently serves on the national board for the Executive Women's Golf Association, the Dallas Chapter Board for The First Tee and the Living Legend Committee for MD Anderson Cancer Center.

She is married and has two children, ages 25 and 27, and lives in Dallas. She is based in Dallas and is currently the senior vice president of member experience for ClubCorp.

CHAPTER 20

Battling Cystic Fibrosis With A Dose of Courage and Golf

By Kim Stanfield

When the idea to put my personal story in writing was first proposed to me, my initial thought was, "No, not me. What do I have to say that would be any different from the next person?"

However, something kept pulling me back to the saved email and a little voice inside of me said, "Do it!" So, this is where my story begins.

Growing up, I was never one to play sports because I have Cystic Fibrosis. I was always the kid in gym class who got picked last for teams.

Having spent much of my childhood and teenage years enduring regular two-week visits in the hospital throughout the year for what we "CFers" call "tune ups," I soon grew to favor academic challenges over physical tests.

Fast forward to my mid-20s, when I have married and am still doing regular "tune ups" to the hospital. At that time, my health had deteriorated so much so that my only option was to have a double-lung transplant. I was fortunate enough to receive my new lungs on Easter Sunday in 1993.

I felt like a new person and began to see my health improve. But my period of good health was short-lived, as I would soon go into renal failure in 1998, due to the transplanted organ rejection medications that I was taking. Now, I needed to undergo a kidney transplant.

So in August 1998, my father volunteered to give me one of his kidneys. Once again, my health improved for a few years until in 2002, when I again went into renal failure. This time, my aunt offered to donate one of her kidneys. What an early Christmas present that was!

It wasn't until 2003 that I first dabbled with the idea of trying to play golf. I wanted to be able to spend more time with my husband and I thought if I had my own clubs, I might enjoy the game. So we bought a set of clubs for me from the local "big box" retail store and I was all set to go.

I soon found out that golf is a difficult game, but I had heard about Natural Golf, which was touted as a simpler way to learn how to play. I felt that I needed to learn the game quicker, so I took some lessons in the Natural Golf technique and became hooked. I soon also ordered custom clubs from Natural Golf, as I am only 4-foot-11 ½ inches tall. It made sense to get clubs to fit my small size.

That all happened in the summer of 2003. My health was finally good and stable, and I thought I would see if there was a fundraising golf tournament for Cystic Fibrosis. My family and I wanted to play in a tournament as a way to give back to the foundation. Besides, back in 1973, I had been the Cystic Fibrosis poster child in Syracuse, N.Y.

So here I was, 30 years later, saying, "Here I am, a success story! Please help the Cystic Fibrosis Foundation!" That was my first year of involvement and in one week before the golf tournament, I was able to raise nearly $10,000 and add five teams with four players per team to the tournament lineup.

The CF Board approached me after the event to see if I would join their committee the following year. That led to a subsequent board position. I was timid for the first couple of years as a golf and committee member, because it was all new to me. But as tournament time rolled around each year, I became more comfortable with the whole event.

When I first began working on the board, I was so shy that I couldn't even ask the tournament players to take their seats for us to start the event. The one year in which it was my responsibility to call all the tournament contestants to order, I froze from fear. And, yes, I was mortified! I vowed to never be in that situation again, so I began participating in a few Toastmasters sessions to overcome my fear of public speaking.

Meanwhile, the golf tournament grew from seven teams of four that first year to 21 teams the next year, and then to a full field of 36 foursomes through my involvement until 2011. We raised an average of $38,000 for the charity (after expenses) each year and elevated the annual CF Tournament back to its original glory days, making it a sought-after tournament entry by golfers of all playing levels.

In the spring of 2006, I saw a flyer for an EWGA golf league at the course where my husband and I like to play. I then decided to try to improve my game and begin league play. I can tell you, I was terrified because I had heard so many horror stories from people in golf leagues. Fortunately, none of them were even close to being true with the local EWGA league that I joined.

As it turned out, joining the EWGA was the best thing I could have done and has helped mold me into the person I am today, both on and off the course. For all who know how to play the game, each of us had to start somewhere – and that somewhere is the beginning. The wonderful women who taught me so much are now my best friends and people I view as life-long friendships.

Also in 2006, after joining my local EWGA league and getting bit by the proverbial "golf bug," I decided I needed more conventional golf instruction and began that journey of learning, which still continues. My experiences with both our local EWGA chapter and the national organization came through attending both the EWGA Championships and the annual conferences. Both have been exceptionally positive experiences.

I was able to advance into the 2009 EWGA Championship finals in Port St. Lucie, Fla. The time spent there was nothing short of amazing. I met many wonderful women from across the country. The following year, I was able to attend the annual conference in Pinehurst, N.C. To say it was a memorable experience would be an understatement. As luck would have it, I was one of the fortunate few to have won a chance to play nine holes on Pinehurst No. 2 with LPGA Hall of Famer Annika Sorenstam.

Annika was the kindest, nicest person and it was truly an honor to have been able to play alongside her that day. The EWGA made that opportunity possible.

Of course, I was really nervous to be playing golf with Annika and right before the round, I was unable to hit a ball because my nerves were getting the best of me. I was one of the players with the highest golf handicaps in the group, but my caddie was awesome and he tried to get me to hit a few shots on the range. We tried all sorts of clubs to help me loosen up and calm down.

Adding to my jangly nerves was the fact this event was happening in April, so I hadn't swung a club all winter prior to this day. It was now almost time to play. We were all introduced to Annika. Somehow, the media found out that Annika was playing at Pinehurst, so the next thing I knew, cameras were showing up all over the place.

When it was my turn to play, I walked up to the tee. To my own surprise, I couldn't get the plastic tee into the ground and when I did, the ball won't stay on the tee. My hands were shaking so much, I had to literally drop my driver to the ground and using *two* hands, put my tee in the ground and steady the ball on the tee. Then, I looked up, saw everyone looking at me and what did I do when I hit the ball? I pull-hooked my tee shot left into the trees of Pinehurst's 10th hole. My caddie calmly said, "It's OK, we can see it and you are OK."

Once we reached the spot where my ball had come to rest, my caddie asked what my favorite club was and I answered that it was my 9-wood. So, my caddie handed it to me. I hit it and the ball flew straight across the fairway and landed in the right rough behind a tree. The media cameramen were right there to film Annika and I was unable to play my next shot because they were so close. My caddie asked them to move back so I could make my swing.

Funny, but I don't remember any other shots that day, although I will never forget the first tee shot. The ranger came up to me after the round and congratulated me on pulling myself together, saying he was quite worried for me on the first tee. I laughed and said, "Me too!" Annika did offer a putting suggestion to me that day. I wanted to show her I was paying attention, but I am embarrassed to say that I three- and four-putted some greens at Pinehurst with her watching. It was quite an experience, to say the least.

Later that same year, during the annual Cystic Fibrosis Golf Tournament – for which we invite and solicit our general contractors, suppliers, family and friends for the event – I decided that I could not greet everyone and also oversee the event as chairperson. So I decided to play a par-3 hole with each team in the tournament.

That meant that with every group, I would tee off, drive my cart over to the green and chip/putt with each team before returning back to the tee to do it all over again with the next group. What I didn't realize was that meant I would be playing 36 holes of golf that day. Yikes! But I managed to do that and we all had a fun time. Needless to say, some teams got a really great tee shot from me while others, well, not so good, but nonetheless, we were all there to raise money for the charity.

To put the icing on the cake for 2010, I qualified for our EWGA Chapter Championship and advanced to compete in the semifinals in Springfield, Mass. I made it through the semifinals and advanced into the EWGA Championship in Lake Geneva, Wis. Playing in the third flight that fall, I saw familiar faces from across the country and felt the camaraderie that I had developed with those great ladies. It was so good to see everyone.

The autumn weather for the national championship was chilly, but my game was present for those two days and I was able to play well enough to win the first low net in the third flight by one stroke. By winning, I earned an exemption into the EWGA Nationals the following year in Palm Springs, Calif.

Needless to say, my golf game didn't travel out west with me. I had a "vanity handicap" because I wanted to see how low I could get it, so I played my home course every weekend and I knew that course like the back of my hand. When I travelled away from my familiar home course, it was a completely different scenario. Maybe the reason I played poorly was the fact we had two snowstorms that autumn and I had played no golf for a month. By the time the national championship was held in Palm Springs, my game was rusty from the layoff from playing.

Looking back on my short history in this game, I can say the uneventful last two years have been great to just be able to play golf. I have also helped out the local EWGA chapter as a board member and served first as a league chairperson, then as an education chairperson, with that term ending in the fall of 2012.

This year, my EWGA involvement was as the 2013 chapter championship director – one I have absolutely loved! We had nearly 50 percent of our membership compete on the day of our chapter championship. The members who did not play served as volunteers, involving 53 percent of our total membership. Hopefully, that trend will continue as we head into next year. Only time will tell, but if I am involved again, I will make it happen!

Until then, I'll just stay focused on continuing to move onward, upward and keep smiling, laughing and, of course, playing golf.

About Kim Stanfield

Kim Stanfield is an outgoing and happy person. She has been married to her husband and sweetheart Gary for 24 years. He has been by her side through many of life's challenges. Her current enjoyment in life is to play golf in the summer and ski in the winter, taking trips to see new places for both sports. Kim is a successful business woman in a man's construction field and enjoys working with her father in the family business to carry it into the 21st century. Philanthropically, she enjoys participating in local Make A Wish fundraisers and has contributed in the past to the local Cystic Fibrosis Foundation and Girl Scouts of America organizations. Her current love of golf has her volunteering for the EWGA Central New York Chapter in various positions. She resides in Syracuse, N.Y.

CHAPTER 21

Bad Shots and Good Breaks: Playing to Your Strengths in the Universal Games of Golf and Life

By Lisa Krouse, Esq., SPHR

In the insurance industry, like so many others, golf plays a very big role in the social aspect of career development, but I didn't truly realize that fact until I turned 50. In my experience, women typically had not been present on the golf course. The reality was that so many of us were balancing our families with our work and our lives. Finding those extra hours on a weekend or during the week to play or practice golf was (or is) next to impossible.

But I was tired of being left out — left out of social events attended by my male colleagues, left out of critical discussions and conversations, left out of decisions I would only learn about on Monday mornings, left out of business-development opportunities. It finally struck me that I was sitting out of the game and in order to continue to succeed, I needed to be in it.

Golf is the closest game to the game we call life.
- Bobby Jones

The first time I decided to participate in a golf event, I signed myself up for a foursome in an invitational that was being sponsored by my company. But something occurred that I had not expected: I was *disinvited* to the event. Heartbroken, I realized that it was either due to my beginner status or that others were trying to protect me from embarrassment. It reminded me of growing up with a disability, trying to ignore the whispers and the sideways glances. I had been the girl who had surgery for her crossed eyes and had to go through the social awkwardness of wearing red glasses and eye patches for a good part of those early years in grade school. Being disinvited to our company's golf event brought back the humiliation I had experienced as a child.

But at that moment, I became determined to improve my game. I had a conversation with Tom Koval. Tom is one of the most influential lawyers in the state of Florida and has a good reputation for his work on the state's workers' compensation laws. He is also an outstanding golfer who will be the first to tell you he has conducted a good many of his negotiations on the golf course. Tom knew I had only recently taken up the game of golf and he seemed surprised when I admitted I was thinking about giving it all up. He pushed to learn why I'd let go of something I had seemed so excited about only a short time ago.

"I'm not a natural," I told him. "I can't seem to get this game. I am mortified that I hold everyone up trying to find my golf balls in the rough or give so many up to water."

"Do one thing before you give it up," said Tom. "Go see Annika Sorenstam."

I laughed. "Learn from the most successful female golfer of all time?" I laughed again. "Oh sure Tom, I'll just give her a call."

But Tom was serious. "She has a golf academy in Orlando and before you give up the game entirely, do me a favor and go."

Tom is generally not one to push. But he is my go-to guy when I need honest advice and support, so I considered his suggestion seriously. "I'll think about it," I told him.

Never let up.
- Sam Snead

Several days later, I enrolled in a weekend clinic at the ANNIKA Academy. Oddly — perhaps good timing, perhaps good luck — I was the only student and Annika's sister, Charlotta Sorenstam, a great golfer in her own right, spent three days working with me. We did one-on-one drills, practice sessions and we played the game out on the course. It didn't appear to me that I was in any way improving, but I was beginning to understand the game better and could see what I needed to work on.

By the second day – and having spent so many hours in the hot sun together – Charlotta and I had established a wonderful rapport. She said something that changed my view of the game forever. She said, "Look Lisa, I have trained my entire life to be No. 2. In fact, I am working on a book that will be entitled just that." Her comment stopped me dead in my swing. And in the way she said it — she seemed so happy, so at peace.

Instantly, I knew her insight would resonate among other women like me. "Do you mind if I use your story in my speeches?" I asked.

"What relevance does my book title have to your speeches?" Charlotta wondered.

"Everything," I said with absolute confidence.

The only thing you can control is your attitude toward the next shot.
- Mark McCumber

Back off the course, I reflected further. As a human resources executive, my focus is on creating a work environment that supports the assumption that employees want to do their very best every day. That's what engagement is all about and we know there is a direct correlation between employee engagement and the success of an organization. A happy employee is a successful employee, and vice versa.

For the next year, my PowerPoint slides highlighted my golf story and how to create a culture of respect and support in the workplace. I incorporated key golf metaphors into the important points I wanted to drive home:

1. Your strategy makes the difference. To be successful in golf, you have to have a strategy before you approach each round. Golfers think long and hard about factors ranging from the direction the wind is blowing, the weather, to the condition of the course. Conditions are rarely perfect.

2. Your stance is critical. Whether analyzing the economy or tackling a workplace challenge, your stance is going to be affected by whatever situation you're in at the moment. Take control and position yourself to succeed.

3. You must keep your focus on the ball. By practicing, making corrections along the way, being open to coaching and being persistent, you can tackle your toughest challenges. Be realistic at each new starting point.

4. Your vision must be broad. Professional golfers use their caddies as collaborative strategists to help them determine what kind of club to use, how to evaluate the conditions, or how big a swing to take. Know where you want to go.

5. You must get tough. One of the most valuable lessons in business is that difficult obstacles can always be overcome. If the ball is in the rough or the mud, get over it and play it as it lies.

As time went on, Charlotta's story took on much deeper meaning for me. It occurred to me that whether you're No. 2 or No. 200, whatever you achieve is about doing your personal best — no matter what that means.

Golf only appears to be a competitive sport because golfers compete against each other, but the true competition in the game of golf is with one's self. In looking to win a round, it's less about capitalizing upon your competitor's weaknesses and more about pursuing a personal best for the win — however that's defined. You are your only competitor. Allowing yourself to focus on another's effort during the round is simply a distraction that wastes the precious resources you need to focus on doing your personal best.

The late, great Raul Julia portrayed an Italian racecar driver in the movie "The Gumball Rally." In one scene, he enters his car, rips the rear view mirror off the windshield and says, "And now my friend, the first-a rule of Italian driving. What's-a behind me is not important."

Golf and life certainly share this truth. A personal best for the hole, the course, the game or your life is about focusing on where you are and what's in front of you. Every stroke — like every career move — represents a new opportunity.

It's a funny thing: the more I practice, the luckier I get.
- Arnold Palmer

Upon my return home from the ANNIKA Academy, I started a women's golf league at my company. I began playing with women who were similarly situated as beginners, as well as women who were quite good. Relationships that might never have been forged were blossoming. Our young professional women were gaining an edge and I saw this as a good thing for them. I was pleased that I was opening a door that, like me, they probably had not realized was traditionally closed.

My team and I continue to benefit from invitations to have business discussions on the golf course. I am also responsible for some of the charitable giving at my organization, which involves several events that revolve around golf. Many of the business relationships I now enjoy so much have become genuine friendships — bonds that will continue to thrive and benefit all parties into the future.

The most important shot in golf is the next one.
-Ben Hogan

That statement, by one of the greatest golfers of all times, really sums up why golf matters. After completing law school, I worked at a legal aid organization for New York's poorest residents. For those who are familiar with the city, the area I worked in is called "Hell's Kitchen."

I remember getting off a New York City bus to visit a client family, looking around and thinking, "This can't be in America." Golf was neither a part of this world, nor a part of mine. I grew up in a very modest home in Brooklyn and I don't ever recall seeing golf on TV or even passing a golf course.

Eventually, when I left New York, I felt like I was carrying the weight of the world on my shoulders. My new life in Florida put me on a positive new career path and I have since had many opportunities to challenge myself. I have worked hard to achieve my own personal best in both life and work — especially through the game of golf. I now understand that I was practicing the principles of golf all along: I had a strategy, I knew when to correct my stance, I kept my focus, I stayed open, and I remained tough.

At this stage of my life, simply being on a golf course — and contrasting my surroundings with my memories of New York — allows me to appreciate the game on a deep level. The beauty of nature, the magnificence of the surrounding solitude, and the connection with people that the golf course demands — all of these bring out a passion for my work, my life and the game of golf.

About Lisa Krouse, Esq., SPHR

Lisa Krouse, Esq., Senior Professional in Human Resources (SPHR), is senior vice president of human resources and support services at FCCI Insurance Group in Sarasota, Fla., a commercial property and casualty insurance company rated A by A.M. Best Company. Prior to joining FCCI, Krouse was general counsel Southeast Region and vice president of human resources at Zenith Insurance Company.

For nearly 10 years, she was vice president and assistant general counsel at National Council on Compensation Insurance, Inc. (NCCI). She was also a partner in the law firm of Adorno & Yoss. She has written for many publications on legal insurance and employment law topics and is a recognized speaker in her area of expertise.

Krouse received her bachelor's degree from New York University and her Juris Doctor from New York Law School. She is admitted to practice before the United States Supreme Court and is a member of the Florida Bar, District of Columbia Bar, and the New York Bar. She sits on the advisory board for the Florida State University College of Business's Center for Human Resource Management and the advisory board of the University of South Florida College of Business.

Krouse spends her free time dedicated to her community. She has served as district director for HR Florida, the state affiliate of the Society for Human Resource Management (SHRM), the world's largest association devoted to human resource management, and as past president of the Sarasota-Manatee Human Resources Association. She spent eight years on the Board of Teen Court of Sarasota, including presiding as a teen-court judge. She was also chair-elect of the Suncoast Workforce Board and a board member for eight years. She currently sits on the Executive Committee of the Greater Sarasota Chamber of Commerce.

CHAPTER 22

Taking the Cart Path to Personal and Professional Growth

By Margaret E. Downey

As I get closer to retirement and reflect on the past, I realize that life can take you down paths that you never expected to travel, both personally and professionally. The same rings true for cart paths.

At the mid-point of my career with CSX Transportation, I was offered an opportunity to accept a promotion and move from Baltimore – my home for the first 36 years of my life – to Jacksonville, Fla. I was excited about the professional opportunity, but also about the change in climate and the opportunity to spend more time on the water. Nothing was better than swimming, fishing or taking a crazy ride being pulled by the boat on an inner tube. At the same time, I was saddened to be leaving behind our extended family, many close friends and a sister who had been a very important part of my life.

When I arrived in Jacksonville, I found myself working for Dennis, a seasoned training professional and an avid golfer. As a big-city girl, I'd never had the opportunity to play golf and knew very little about the sport, but about six months after my arrival, that would all change.

Dennis soon sent out an announcement about the annual staff meeting at his country club and I was surprised to learn that we would all be expected to play 18 holes of golf at the conclusion of the business meeting. I have to admit that I was quite nervous about the meeting. I was the "new kid on the team," but also very unsure about golf. My only minutely relevant experience had been several rounds of miniature golf at Jungle Land during our annual family vacation.

The day of the staff meeting was a fabulously sunny, fall day. When I pulled into the Jacksonville Golf & Country Club parking lot, I was pleasantly surprised by the beautiful surroundings. The clubhouse had a wide porch that wrapped around the entire building and the landscaping and flowers were breathtaking. But nothing was more spectacular than the view from the back of the building that took in most of the 9th and 18th holes, separated by a beautiful pond full of Canada geese. Most of the meeting was held on the back porch, and as the day progressed I found it harder and harder to concentrate as the presenter droned on about theories of adult learning.

After lunch we were given some time to "warm up" for the afternoon's golf activities. Darrell, my work colleague, had been kind enough to loan me his wife's old set of clubs. As I carried them over to the driving range, I watched the experienced players on our staff easily hit balls. Darrell gave me a quick rundown of the equipment in the golf bag and handed me a bucket of range balls.

As I started to give it a try, it didn't take me long to understand that there was much more to a golf swing than I had realized. I was lucky enough to hit several balls about 100 yards and I was sure I'd figure it out as the day wore on. Finally, the event organizer called us over to the practice green and announced the teams for the afternoon. I was surprised to learn that I would be playing with my boss, Dennis. Since he was a professional trainer, I was sure that he'd be patient and give me some tips that would help me learn to hit the ball more confidently.

After playing the first couple of holes, it was quite obvious that I had no idea what I was doing. I lacked even the basic fundamentals of a golf swing and didn't understand any of the rules or etiquette of the game. It also became apparent that Dennis was a strong player and quite competitive, with every intention of posting the best score of the afternoon for his team.

The patience that I hoped he would possess was nowhere to be found! He actually became quite impatient and would count the number of times that I whiffed my tee shots, almost like strikes against a batter at home plate. The harder I tried, the worse it got. If there was anything positive that came from that long and agonizing afternoon, it was my intent to never find myself in the same situation again. I made a personal promise to take some lessons and learn the basics of golf before the next staff meeting in the spring.

Fortunately for me, there was a chapter of the Executive Women's Golf Association (EWGA) forming in Jacksonville. Several women at CSX were part of the organizing group and I was asked to join the committee. I became a founding member of the chapter and the networking chairwoman the first year. That spring, I was the first one to sign up for beginner lessons, along with two other CSX women named Kathy and Rose Marie, whom I knew casually from Baltimore. We attended our weekly lessons and began to practice together.

The three of us were intent on learning and made a new friend with a retired AT&T executive named Dorothy. Dorothy believed that golf was an important business tool for professional women and took us under her wing. We would go each Saturday morning to the Palm Valley practice course and Dorothy would instruct us on rules and etiquette, and we eventually "graduated" to playing 18 holes together at many of the wonderful golf courses in the area. Before long, we became close friends and we called Dorothy our "golf-mother," because she shared what she knew about golf, its importance as a business tool and her experiences as a business executive.

This newfound path that life had taken me down – this cart path – soon became an important part of my life. I was hooked on the game and the lifestyle that surrounded golf. As I traveled down this cart path over the next 18 years, my life would be influenced in many ways by the game, the opportunities it would present, the people I would meet and the new and strengthened relationships that would be formed. In reflection, here's what I can share that will help you "Tee it up for Success":

1. **Golf will help you build your network.** Rarely at a traditional networking event do you have more than a few minutes to speak to someone. If you do, it's the usual exchange of names, employers and other superficial information. Playing golf with someone gives you the unique opportunity to spend several uninterrupted hours together. You'll also learn a great deal about a playing partner's personality – much more than you could learn over lunch or a brief exchange at a networking event.

2. **Golf is an important tool to have in your toolbox.** It can set you apart from others. This is especially easy for women who play golf, since it's rare to find more than a handful of women at a corporate tournament or charity event. I've seen many lists of the top-10 skills important for business success for women and golf is often on these lists. It will also help you form bonds with your male colleagues. I've had many work relationships strengthened with my male counterparts through the game of golf. They will develop a new appreciation for you as an individual when you display honesty, integrity, sportsmanship and other important traits that are a part of golf.

3. **Golf teaches us that we all have handicaps.** Both successes and failures are temporary and there is much to learn in both situations. Just as we strive to reduce our golf handicap, we strive to reduce our mistakes and become stronger from the lessons of life.

4. **Golf builds confidence.** It's a difficult sport to learn, so once you begin to master it your confidence grows. You are ready to play business golf when you can hit the ball consistently and are comfortable with the etiquette and rules of the game.

5. **Golf is a family sport.** It's a lifetime sport mixed with travel and fun for the whole family. It offers a time when you can create strong bonds by getting away to spend time together, while having quality

conversation and enjoying beautiful surroundings. Your children and grandchildren can learn focus, patience and how to handle challenges while playing golf. You're also investing in their skill development, since playing the game may help them professionally in the future.

6. **Friendships are more important than always having the winning score.** Don't always get caught up in winning the bet or posting the lowest score. The joy that comes from a deep pool of friends far outweighs being known as the best player in the group. Take time to listen and enjoy those with whom you are fortunate enough to play. Some of my dearest friends are the women whom I have encountered through golf – either as playing partners or volunteers working for various golf-related charities or associations.

7. **Volunteerism creates great opportunities to learn new skills.** Being a 20-year volunteer with the EWGA has enriched my life and helped me develop many new skills — skills in leadership, public speaking, strategic planning and business finance. It's important that you can find a place where you can give and learn at the same time.

8. **Golf can help you make a difference in the lives of others.** The women who helped me learn to play golf and use it as a business tool have also created a desire in me to give back through the game of golf. There are wonderful organizations that use golf to teach life skills to children. Two of my favorites are The First Tee and the LPGA/USGA Girls Golf Programs. Golf can also be used as a wonderful tool for fundraising for whatever charities you desire to support. The important thing is to make a difference in whatever you choose to do.

I hope this short chapter about my experiences with golf will encourage other young women to invest in their future by learning to play and leverage golf as an important business tool. The cart path that I have traveled has provided a wonderfully fulfilling ride, both personally and professionally. As I start to prepare for retirement, I want to leverage the lessons that golf has taught me and give back through the game in whatever way that I can.

About Margaret Downey

Margaret Downey is a human resources professional with more than 25 years experience in her field. She is a native of Baltimore, Md., but has lived in Jacksonville, Fla. for 20-plus years. She is a graduate of Jacksonville University, where she earned her M.B.A. in 1999.

She is a long-tenured employee of CSX Transportation and currently serves in the role of general manager, learning & development strategies where she sets direction and oversees the development and implementation of learning and development programs. Her most significant accomplishment is the design, construction and staffing of a $28 million training facility in Atlanta called the Railroad Education & Development Institute. More than 30,000 railroad workers have attended training at REDI since it opened in 2005.

Margaret also is an adjunct faculty member at Webster University, where she teaches in the master's program for human resources development. She has been a member of their faculty since 2000, and enjoys working with adult students pursuing advanced degrees.

She currently serves on the board of directors for the First Coast Business Leadership Network, an organization that advocates for jobs for persons with disabilities. She is active in the golf community and serves on the board of directors and executive committee for The First Tee of North Florida and is the president of the board of directors of the Executive Women's Golf Association.

CHAPTER 23

Once Reluctant Golfer Now Finds Joy In the Game, Value in the Business Tool

By Mitzi Short

I love this game! And I have been fortunate enough to see some of the world's most beautiful and prestigious golf courses, such as the Old Course at St. Andrews, Pebble Beach Golf Links and Pinehurst Resort.

I have played in pro-am golf tournaments with some of the LPGA and PGA's most recognizable golf professionals, including Meg Mallon, Patty Sheehan, Rosie Jones, Fred Couples and David Duval. I watched Tiger Woods play in the U.S. Open Championship at Pebble Beach from the gallery and from the stands. I even had the late Earl Woods, Tiger's father, participate as the keynote speaker at one of my annual facility kick-off meetings. Not bad for someone who did not initially know golf, right?

Despite being born and growing up less than 10 miles from Upper Arlington, Ohio – the hometown of Jack Nicklaus, one of golf's most famous sons – I did not play golf as a child. My friends also did not play golf. In fact, I did not know anyone who played golf until I met my college roommate as a sophomore.

Fortunately, my connection to golf began to change when I graduated from Davidson College in North Carolina and started my career in sales at Procter & Gamble. At work, my introduction to golf came quickly. Golf almost seemed to be woven into the fabric of Corporate America's extra-curricular activities. I found golf at sales conferences, customer functions and in team-building activities. My colleagues played golf, my bosses played golf and so did my customers.

I quickly learned that customers were serious about their golf. During a customer meeting at Oregon Golf Club, I learned just how serious they were. I was the new Pepsi Cola General Manager in Portland, Ore., and I was being introduced to one of our larger customers. We were going to play golf and our foursome consisted of my lead salesman, two customer leaders and me.

Rain clouds hung overhead for our round and it started to drizzle, so I began to pack up my belongings to take cover. I was amazed that no one else in the foursome seemed to notice as the drizzle became big raindrops and then a torrential downpour. It was not the thunder or lightning, but *only* the insistence of the course ranger that prompted our customers to finally "call it a round" and go in.

My bosses also enjoyed golf and golf conversations. Consequently, I worked hard to know who the key players were in the game, who was winning the week's professional tournaments and how to speak the language of golf. Sometimes, I tried too hard. I had a boss whose last name was Sheehan. I did not know many Sheehans and after playing in a pro-am golf tournament with LPGA Hall of Famer Patty Sheehan, I presumed she was his sister. In my attempts to connect with him and impress him with my knowledge of the game, I would often weave Patty Sheehan updates into our conversations. I was so intent on connecting with him that I missed his comments about them not being related. We joked about that for a while.

Since golf was a key part of the corporate culture, it did not take long to figure out that I needed to learn more about playing golf. Admittedly, I dreaded the thought. From my limited perspective, I thought golf was slow and boring. I worked in an environment where producing solid business performance mattered the most. So, I was keenly focused on delivering stellar results in order to meet my bosses' expectations and continue to advance my career. How could I possibly waste four hours chasing a little white ball around a golf course? Why spend an entire afternoon on the golf course to discuss what I could easily cover in 30-45 minutes? What was the point?

My initial foray into golf was merely to go to the course as a work assignment. I would work in the clubhouse until it was time for the golfers to return to the clubhouse from their rounds. I would then greet them enthusiastically, asking how the round went and check to see if everyone had a wonderful time. I would try to inject myself into what was often the conversation at the end of the day. To my dismay, I felt out of touch because I was not part of the main conversations. My effort to share their experience was a weak attempt at "being present" — like dipping my toe into the ocean and saying that I had tried scuba diving. I soon realized I had to revise my plan.

My next attempt at increased involvement was to be the "designated driver" of a golf cart. As the designated driver, I thought I could be present and perhaps no one would know that I actually did not play golf. Well, that did not work, either. It was torture. While I loved the first-hand participation in conversations, I was not at all thrilled with being in the gallery. I wanted to be in the game where the action was! After all, I was a former high school and collegiate athlete, having played on a state high school basketball championship runners-up team and on a collegiate regional field hockey championship squad. How hard could golf be?

Based on my athletic background, I assumed that golf would be easy to learn. It did not look that difficult to play. At first, I tried to learn how to play on my own with a few sporadic professional lessons. This was not my best idea. I can vividly remember a few painfully embarrassing situations during my days as a golf novice.

On one occasion, while playing at a customer golf tournament, I hit a ball onto a porch of a golf-course home and it ricocheted off *every* piece of patio furniture and landed at the homeowner's feet. It was pretty obvious to him – and to the bystanders who gathered to see what all the noise was about – that I was the culprit. The homeowner knew it had to be me. The logo on my golf shirt matched the logo on the ball that he was holding in his hand.

Then, there was the time, at another well-attended customer event, when one of my errant golf shots hit a deer. For the rest of the day and at every subsequent golf tournament that included members of that foursome, I was nicknamed and referred to as the "Bambi Killer."

As I moved up the corporate ladder, golf continued to be a mainstay of many customer and charity fundraising events. The stakes got higher for me as I was being paired in foursomes with more senior leaders. I was intimidated by the imagined golf prowess of my potential foursomes. For some unsubstantiated reason, I figured the more senior the leader, the lower their average golf score would be. I did not want to embarrass my company or myself. I felt my golf game needed to be respectable. Clearly, I needed to change my approach to learning how to play.

A key turning point came during a vacation to Scotland. I played a round of golf with college friends and family at the historic Old Course in St. Andrews. I lost more balls and played out of more bunkers that were taller than me than I care to remember. Yet, as I played at St. Andrews, revered as "the home of golf," I realized how much I really loved to play the game and how much I valued the camaraderie and connections forged on the golf course. I also realized that I should cherish the experience and work on my game, since I had been blessed with the opportunity to play some of the world's best golf courses.

It was time to execute a new strategy. I became very serious and intentional about improving my golf game. My mantra became: Take professional lessons and play often. I took professional lessons at GolfTEC with PGA Professional Ty Walker. I was intrigued by GolfTEC's high-tech lessons. I loved their private instructional bays because no one could see how poorly I played while I was working to get better.

As I got better and my love for the game increased, I introduced golf to some of the people I love the most. I got my brothers hooked by showing them how much fun the game can be and how it could help their careers. Now, the lowest golf score (usually mine) has replaced the highest bowling score in determining sibling bragging rights in our family! I lured my dad into playing by espousing the benefits of life-long exercise and showing him it was a great way to spend quality time with family and friends of all ages. I also joined the Executive Women's Golf Association so I could play more and network with other professional businesswomen.

After much focus and practice, I now have a respectable golf game. Gone are the days when my scorecard resembled a "frosty the snowman" convention with so many 8s. I have progressed from the embarrassing days of picking up my ball because I had reached the maximum shots allowed per hole. Now, I have chances for birdie putts or a few turbo-powered drives off the tee during tournaments. I can reminisce now with colleagues and clients about top-three tournament finishes, a customer tournament championship and even an eagle at Sahalee Country Club in Sammamish, Wash.

I knew I was hooked when my motivation for playing shifted from seeing golf as something I had to do, rather than something I really enjoyed doing. I found myself proactively integrating golf into my life on more occasions. And, I gained insight on leadership through golf. It helped teach me how to better cultivate relationships and broker deals, how to be more patient and it helped me better understand the power of being present.

Through golf, I also learned the benefit of being focused, the balance between risk and reward and the importance of being resilient. I also gained confidence and found a forum to create the life that I imagined – to "put feet on my prayers," as my grandmother would say.

My life has been enriched by the many experiences and opportunities I have had due to my association with golf. I see many parallels between business, life and the game of golf. In fact, there are similarities in how I play the game and the way I live my life with ***G***oals, ***O***ptimism, an attempt to ***L***ive without regret and to have ***F***un.

Now, I truly love this game! I am grateful to those who paved the way and appreciative of the many who mentored and coached me along the course, both in golf and in business.

About Mitzi Short

Mitzi Short is an adjunct executive coach with the Center for Creative Leadership and co-founder and managing partner of New Season Coaching & Consulting Group – a multi-faceted management consulting and coaching firm specializing in executive leadership and personal coaching, organizational effectiveness, talent management and diversity and inclusion strategy.

As a certified executive leadership and productivity coach, Short works with corporate and organization leaders and professionals who want to maximize their impact, effectiveness and influence in national and global organizations. She is passionate about helping individuals achieve optimal performance and sustainable growth, while living and leading balanced lives.

Her experience spans 25-plus years with Fortune 50 Companies PepsiCo and Procter & Gamble, where she held leadership roles in sales, marketing, operations and general management. She earned her M.B.A. from the University of Oregon, her bachelor's degree in economics from Davidson College and her coaching credentials from the Center for Creative Leadership, the Coaching & Positive Psychology (CaPP) Institute and at the Institute of Integrative Nutrition.

Short's commitment extends to her community, where she chairs the Davidson College Trustee Admissions and Financial Aid Committee and is a member of The Executive Leadership Council, The Executives' Club of Chicago and GolfTEC's Advisory Board. She has been a panelist and featured speaker at conferences, corporate and government events and community programs. She is also a member of the Chicago Metro Chapter of the Executive Women's Golf Association (EWGA) and the owner of several GolfTEC Improvement Centers. Short enjoys photography, playing golf and traveling and currently resides in Oak Park, Ill.

CHAPTER 24

The Power of a Dimpled Ball

By Pam Swensen

A golf ball. It's dimpled. It's 1.68 inches in diameter and weighs a maximum of 1.62 ounces. It can be any color and has 336 dimples. So what? Well, it's been a game changer for me. During my career in the golf industry, I have more stories than dimples on the golf ball!

I didn't grow up in a golf household. My hometown of Brockton, Mass., was a middle class manufacturing town outside Boston. Scholarships earned through beauty pageant wins and part time jobs all contributed to my Skidmore College tuition.

It wasn't until I was out of college working in advertising for a telecommunications company in Boston when golf entered my life. Deregulation had just hit the telecom industry and the company I worked for could no longer take business for granted. They needed to engage creatively with their clients. My CEO was an avid golfer and tapped me to roll out a client entertainment program for our business units, which focused on golf.

Since I didn't play golf, I needed to learn about the sport. I'd heard about this group called EWGA in Boston. So I joined. As women, we don't want to embarrass ourselves and we also want to know what we are getting into, before we jump in – right? EWGA helped me learn the basics and get started – who would have ever imagined where that would lead.

The golf industry is challenging, but I like challenges. It's a male-dominated industry and is still largely led by middle-aged white guys. So, I've had to work really hard to prove myself.

When I left telecommunications, I went to work for a golf marketing company led by female professional golfer, Jane Blalock. I became the face of her company, JBC Golf. I went to industry functions, networked, volunteered to serve on industry committees, all while increasing my profile, so I would be known and respected for my accomplishments. I had the opportunity to work with several Fortune 500 clients during this time, managing their corporate golf programs.

On one occasion, I was playing golf at Pebble Beach Resorts with some clients and one of our caddies was nicknamed "Foot." I really didn't get it at first. However, after several holes, my ball was always in great position and I began to question it because I knew my shots weren't all that good. Other people in my foursome were also playing exceptionally well and didn't seem to mind the assistance of the caddie.

When he said to me, "They don't call me 'Foot' for nothing, you know," I was mortified. What about golf's core values? What about honesty, integrity, sportsmanship, honor and respect? While this experience really opened my eyes, it also reinforced the valuable traits you can witness on the golf course about yourself and your playing partners.

Golf has allowed me to build a career within the golf industry. I've built relationships among titans of industry and among marquee players. It has opened doors for me to play golf in pro-ams with legends of yesterday and superstars of today, on both the men's and women's circuits. It has enabled me to lead an organization that has touched the lives of more than 120,000 women in our 22-year history.

One fond memory goes back to being a pro-am guest of an EWGA member at a LPGA tournament. At that time, the pro-am pairings party actually was an electronic draw. We drew the second pick. The first group picked Christina Kim. Our choices were Annika Sorenstam, Paula Creamer, Morgan Pressel, Lorena Ochoa and Cristie Kerr – all the top stars of the LPGA. We chose Annika! We were so excited and were high-fiving and looking forward in anticipation to the next day's experience.

After our excitement came the realization that we were going to tee it up with the No. 1 female golfer in the world! Pam Swensen was going to be paired with Annika Sorenstam! Four holes into the round, Annika asked if I minded some advice. I had been spraying my shots to the left and right, so I said, "Sure!" After she removed her belt and tied it around my arms to stop my flying elbow, I was humbled and began concentrating so intensely on my shot execution that I was exhausted by the end of the round – in an exhilarating kind of way. From that experience, we (EWGA) have partnered with Annika and her businesses on numerous occasions and I have co-hosted several Women's Day events with her. It's through golf that this relationship was possible.

Golf is a connector. It offers you a relationship-building skill that opens doors. It opens doors to business opportunities, to terrific venues and opens doors to what you are truly made of. And by this I mean personal qualities that define who you are and how you translate your image, actions and abilities in real life. It defines you as a person. It allows others to see what type of person you are in good times, in adverse and challenging conditions and it's all part of an 18-hole round of golf.

One day, my phone rang and the voice on the other end said, "I'm Marty Carr from Ireland and I'll be in West Palm Beach next week. I'd like to come and meet with you about the 2011 Solheim Cup." That was just the beginning. The Carr family is Irish golf royalty. His dad, Joe Carr, is in the World Golf Hall of Fame. His brother, Rodney, is well known in international golf player representation and tournament management circles. I've played at Wayne Huizenga's Floridian Club with the Carr brothers, met Mr. Huizenga at a breakfast there, launched EWGA-Bermuda with Rodney's help and yes, we organized a trip with Carr Golf for more than 250 EWGA members to Ireland. Carr Golf has been a sponsor of EWGA conferences. This is about connections, relationships and door openers, all a result of the critical golf tool – that dimpled ball!

When I was invited to play in the Allianz Championship Pro-Am, I was one of a few women present that day. Warming up on the range with the guys pounding their drives 300-plus yards took inner strength. My golf bag (bright kelly green with white stripes) stood out from the sea of black golf bags at the bag-drop area. As I started to warm up, I looked to my right and saw Paul Azinger (former U.S. Ryder Cup team captain) hitting balls. My first thought was, why was he at this end of the range hitting with all of the amateurs and not at the other end with the PGA TOUR players? Then, I thought, "I hope I don't take him out with an errant swing!" I stopped warming up, went over to him and introduced myself. He was quite gracious even though he wasn't my pro for that day.

Olin Browne was my professional for this event. It just so happened that his daughter was dating Rickie Fowler, who was, at that time, the new rookie phenom on the PGA TOUR. I was quite nervous being the only woman in the group. Our first hole was a par- 3 hole and yes, there was a gallery present. Fortunately, I landed my tee shot on the green and was the only amateur in the group to par the hole. And we were off! I felt my confidence soar and spent the round getting to know Olin better, learning about how he viewed this dating relationship, while the three other men in my group were interested in the power of their drivers and what clubs to use to recover from their errant shots. It was a fabulous time.

There's a cartoon I saw several years ago in the Wall Street Journal that I have never forgotten. It depicted two people discussing a potential new hire for their office. The caption was, "Her qualifications are excellent, good references, five years practical experience – and she shoots in the low 80s".

Playing golf changed my life. I did have mentors – both male and female – who encouraged me to serve on committees, to speak and to demonstrate a willingness to be a leader. Now as the face of EWGA, I make it a priority to be present and visible at as many industry golf events as possible. I am always looking to go the distance in delivering a clear, positive message about why women need to play golf and how the industry should roll out the green carpet to this extremely powerful consumer segment.

One day, I received an email from a female golf professional in Kenya. She was looking for assistance for her girls' golf school. Her name was Rose Naliaka. When I read her email and considered her request for donations of golf supplies for her girls – who by the way, were shoeless and truly lived in sub-par conditions – I thought to myself, if an organization like EWGA can't help her, who will?

So, this started our Drive for Dreams program to provide resources for those in need. Through that program, we were able to offer golf clubs, balls, bags, shoes, clothing, personal-care items, video cameras and whatever we could collect to assist her. The story is still ongoing. Rose now has one of the top amateur golfers in Kenya under her tutelage. We assisted Rose with travel to the United States to receive her LPGA Class A Teaching Certification. She has taken her girls, through generous donations and connections she has made through her EWGA network, to St. Andrews to the British Women's Open.

Rose has also been introduced to Betsy King, who has also visited Rose in Kenya. This story demonstrates what a great door opener and connector golf can be and how it can truly change lives. When I told the owners of SNAG Golf Rose's story, they immediately wanted to help her with additional learning tools for her school. Now, we are talking about starting an EWGA chapter in Kenya. Changing lives and truly making a difference for Rose's girls and their future is what it's all about. Once again, it's about relationships.

Maya Angelou once said, "I've learned that people will forget what you said, people will forget what you did, but people will never forget how you made them feel," and isn't that the crux of developing a relationship with someone?

So, I share this with you. Relationships are, indeed, born on the golf course and through golf. And it's not just a dimpled golf ball – or even a crystal ball. For me, it's been a pot of gold!

I encourage all of you to test the waters. See what doors golf can open for you. Join us! Consider this my personal invitation. I've met women who have the potential to change the course of my life – and have! You can also experience that.

Thanks to EWGA for providing me a gateway and an environment to make me more confident in what I do to enrich women's lives through the game of golf.

About Pam Swensen

Pam Swensen, CEO of the Executive Women's Golf Association (EWGA), is the "face" of EWGA to the golf industry. Her leadership enables current and aspiring business and professional women to learn, connect and play—through golf – using the power of its 14,000-plus membership with their $66 million impact on the game to create new opportunities for current and future members.

With this "power of the purse influence," Swensen represents the EWGA on several industry committees to grow the game and advocates for issues that will make the women's golf experience more welcoming. She's a member of the Golf 20/20 Executive Committee, a founding member of the National Women's Golf Alliance, a member of EWomen Network's Foundation Advisory Council, the USGA Regional Associations Committee, The Women's Chamber of The Palm Beaches, The American Society of Association Executives, the Florida Society of Association Executives, and The Commonwealth Institute Forum Group. She also serves on the International Network of Golf Advisory Board and is a member of the Palm Beach County Chapter of the EWGA.

Swensen is the recipient of a Mover & Shaker Award from Golf Inc. Magazine and was honored with a "Giraffe" Award from the Women's Chamber of the Palm Beaches, which recognizes women who have "stuck their necks out" in making a difference to other women in the workplace and in the community. She's been recognized by the African American Golfer's Digest with an Outstanding Leaders in Golf award and was honored with the Trainor Award from the LPGA Futures Tour for the EWGA's work in growing women's golf.

She holds a bachelor's degree from Skidmore College and a master's degree in communications from Boston University.

CHAPTER 25

Rounds On the Links Created Links Financial

By Penny Larsen

After working for more than 20 years in Corporate America, I started my own business nearly eight years ago. I never thought that I would become an entrepreneur, but the businesswomen I met while playing golf advised, counseled and inspired me to set out on my own.

My sister and I were taught to play golf at a young age by my mother, who played golf with some of the other neighborhood moms. I played on and off throughout my teens and in college when time and money to play permitted. At the time, I looked at the game as something to do recreationally with a friend, boyfriend or my sister.

About the same time that I became more focused on my career aspirations, I learned about an organization that was forming. It was called the Executive Women's Golf League. (The name was later changed to the Executive Women's Golf Association and now simply, EWGA.) The purpose of the group was to help businesswomen learn to play the game of golf, as well as to provide a network of other women golfers.

As one of the original 28 people who formed the organization, I have been involved my entire adult life. All of the major events that have shaped my life have been associated or influenced by the lifelong friendships and business-women I've met through the organization. I loved the social aspects of the game, especially the camaraderie and the friendships that were made after playing 18 holes of golf. The women I met became my best friends as we celebrated weddings, job promotions and babies born.

As a math and business major in college, I was fascinated by the world of banking and I knew that I wanted to become a commercial banker to help businesses borrow money to expand and grow. To this day, I can hear my very Southern mother say, "I can't believe that I have a daughter who is good at math. I can't even add my golf score and it isn't that high!"

But I loved working with numbers and figures and was fascinated by the banking industry. Upon graduation, I went to work for a very large commercial bank and stayed with the company for almost 20 years. I never thought that I would work anywhere else and that I would eventually retire from that same company – but that didn't happen.

My father worked for the United States Government for his entire career. Although he was often asked to join the companies who had military and defense contracts with which he interacted, he never did because his era believed that workers were loyal to their employers and stayed until retirement. And that was the way I was taught, too. But as this was not to be for me, I ended up working for two other large commercial banks, where, in my last position, I served as their regional president for the Tampa Bay area in Florida.

After leaving that bank, I was at a crossroad for what waited ahead. Would I take another regional position being offered by yet another bank or try something else? Just as other wage-earning workers have often foolishly said, I thought, "It's easy to start a business, and entrepreneurs make much more money than they deserve."

As a commercial banker, I was privy to the financial statements of numerous privately held businesses and that information often included the salaries of those business owners. As brash young bankers, my colleagues and I would often look on the paperwork for where the business owner's salary was listed and make silly statements like, "We are just as smart and talented as that business owner, so why aren't we making that kind of money?"

Of course by the time we were introduced to these business owners, they would have likely had well-established businesses with lengthy track records. We weren't around at the formation of those companies, when that well-paid business owner didn't know if his company would survive – or if his new product launch would be successful, or if her competition was going to be successful in putting her out of business. What we saw was the result of the huge risk the business owner had taken and that it had all worked out. What none of my fellow bankers and I recognized is that it takes a huge amount of courage to start a business, and none of us had the guts to do it.

As I was pondering what to do next, I played a lot of golf in the meantime. (In case you are wondering, your short game really will improve if you play a lot of golf!) In addition to improving my iron play, I spent time considering other job offers and made a half-hearted attempt at creating a list of the pros and cons that each one offered. I thought this would help me pick the best alternative – all the while, trying to avoid what, in my heart, I knew that I should do next.

I kept pretending that one of those job offers would be the one, but in the meantime, I kept playing golf and volunteering with the Executive Women's Golf Association. Those businesswomen I had met through the EWGA were providing me with helpful advice and suggestions as we played a round or set up a charity tournament. And, those women helped me find the courage to start my own business – Links Financial LLC.

The purpose of my company was, and is, to help business owners either find a lender to help them grow their business or to negotiate with the current lender to help them restructure their debts. Links Financial LLC assists growing and midsize business owners, real estate developers and investors in obtaining debt financing. Because of the time spent with those commercial banks, my experience, expertise and commitment guide my understanding of clients and their business needs. And, through long-established business relations within the financial community, my company has been able to provide our clients an immediate introduction to customized financial resources to meet their specific capital needs.

In addition to sourcing new debt, Links Financial assists borrowers in restructuring their company and their existing debt. Our goal is to help borrowers avoid costly litigation and ensure a successful turnaround of a company's operations and financial picture. I am proud to say that with Links Financial as the financial advocate, our borrower clients have been successful in obtaining their desired outcome – whether it was to minimize a personal guaranty or lessen their debt obligations.

I can now easily describe what my company is and does and I feel excited about its future, but it was certainly scary when I started! I had no idea how to get started. I knew what I wanted to do, but I didn't know about the basic things – like what should I name my business and how to set up a website. And that first time I had to make payroll – wow! Whether or not the company earns a dime, I still had to pay rent, fund payroll and cover the expenses. But, once again, my golf buddies were there for me with advice and support.

At the start, I remember trying out various names and logos with numerous golf friends. Because of my love for the game and the assistance I was getting from my golf buddies, I wanted a company name that would somewhat describe my business and tie into golf, which is not easy to do. I almost went with the name Pinnacle Financial, but one fellow golfer told me the name sounded too much like golf balls – and it was not her favorite brand, either.

At one of the seminars I attended through the EWGA, I heard a marketing expert say that using a name that has the "K" sound makes for a good name. Eventually my EWGA "village" and I decided that the Links name would connote what the business does – "link up" borrowers and lenders, as well as pay tribute to the game that we love.

Others had to help me with my public relations, website and my employee issues. Although I had hired and fired numerous people at prior companies,

I had never really *hired* anyone – meaning, I'd never completed the entire process because the personnel department had taken care of that. In the past, all I had to do was select the candidate that I wanted to hire.

So, someone had to help me create an application form and establish a hiring process for Links Financial. And I remember when, on my company's third anniversary, one of my golf buddies called to congratulate me and to tell me that I was now "officially unemployable." I didn't understand what she meant, so as a fellow business owner, she told me that once I was in business for myself for three years, I could never go back to working for someone else!

Through the creation, formation and beginning of my business, my golf friends were there for me. They believed in me and helped push me to believe in myself. They also pushed me to have the guts to follow my dream.

I truly believe the key to my business success came from all of my golf buddies telling me and reinforcing the message that I really could make it and become a successful entrepreneur. They helped me build the bridge from the links to my business, making this round of my career a fulfilling journey.

About Penny Larsen

Spanning a professional career of more than 25 years, Penny Larsen has worked for top firms in the financial services industry. Her focus has been debt financing, financial management and consulting, project and process management, team and leadership development and problem loan resolution.

Larsen earned a bachelor's degree in mathematics and business, graduating cum laude at Wake Forest University. She also earned her MBA with a finance concentration from the University of Tampa, graduating with top honors. Prior to founding Links Financial LLC, her banking career has included senior positions with Bank of America, Northern Trust and the Royal Bank of Canada's U.S. subsidiary.

Her professional affiliations include: Association for Corporate Growth; University of Tampa; CEO Council of Tampa; Make-A-Wish Foundation; Trinity Café; Commercial Real Estate Women of Tampa Bay; Executive Women's Golf Association; and the American Cancer Society.

Links Financial LLC is a mortgage broker business and Larsen is a licensed mortgage broker and a real estate sales associate.

Her company is a financial intermediary firm that provides two main services: debt financings and debt restructurings. Links Financial helps its clients borrow money. Larsen identifies the most appropriate financing product for the client, provides referrals to funding sources and advocates for the client during the process. For debt restructurings, the company negotiates with current lenders to find the best solution for problem loans. Larsen has successfully negotiated more than $50 million in debt forgiveness for her borrower clients within the last year.

CHAPTER 26

Using the "Little Engine" For Golf and Business

By Priscilla Hill-Ardoin

I do not remember the specific details of the first time I heard the story of *The Little Engine That Could*. I can only imagine that it must have been during a very formative period of my life.

Whenever it was, that refrain of *The Little Engine* chugging along saying, "I think I can, I think I can...I know I can," has influenced my approach to many personal and professional undertakings. It most certainly was the impetus that gave me the courage to pick up a golf club and take a swing at that little white ball.

My first foray into golf was the result of a friend inviting me to join her and a group of co-workers at the driving range to "hit some balls." While I had been with my company for almost two decades, I had recently relocated and taken a new position. The invitation offered an opportunity to get to know a group of colleagues and to learn more about what was happening across the company.

There was no question that, indeed, I could join them on the driving range. Whether or not I could actually "HIT some balls" was highly questionable, given the fact that I had never held a golf club. However, in true Little Engine spirit, I responded, "Of course, I can!"

It ended up being a great evening. My tenacious nature, aggressive spirit and the Callaway women's 7-iron loaned to me, served me well, as I was able to make solid contact with the ball. Of course, where my shots went was an altogether different story, but that experience was the beginning of a wonderful confluence of memorable events that golf would offer in my life.

Quality Family Time (QFT)

I can't tell you how excited I was to go home and tell my husband and sons what fun I'd had on my golf excursion! My 13-year-old son was not shy in letting me know that ONE trip to a driving range did not really qualify as a "golf excursion." Just as my prideful chest was about to deflate, my 15-year-old son added that he was confident I would be able to play golf well if I took lessons.

I immediately signed our family of four up for a class of six lessons offered through the local community college. What started out as one hour, one day a week, quickly turned into taking golf lessons accompanied by another hour or two a week of practice. Our golf lessons quickly morphed into a truly bonding experience for our family.

As a working mother, I often felt guilty that the demands of the job I loved (working long hours, staying late in the office, travel, business obligations in the evening, etc.) kept me away from the sons I adored and loved more. Golf did not make any of those demands go away, however, it did assuage my guilt and provide me with some much enjoyed QFT – Quality Family Time, as it was called in my family.

Golf was never really a sport for me, but instead, a three-to-four-hour span of time spend outdoors together in beautiful environments in which we would talk, eat, laugh, compete against each other, coach each other and simply be together. Spending those few hours together as a family for those sessions were precious times, not to mention that I was finally doing something that my guys thought was cool!

Best of Times with the Best

Less than a year after I first wrapped my fingers around the grip of a golf club, I found myself back at corporate headquarters in a new position with a diverse portfolio of responsibility that included all corporate golf activities. Eager to get on board with the new position, I decided to attend a company-sponsored golf event to see just what all was involved.

My support staff advised that I should arrive early to this event so I could get a feel for everything that would take place – from the preparation to execution. I did just that.

I was astonished at the amount of real work that goes into preparing for a corporate golf event and was impressed with the professional manner in which the team executed their duties to make this event a success.

I knew this was going to be a good assignment when the team finished their work early the evening before the tournament would begin and a few of us headed to the driving range. I had positioned myself at the driving range, placed the ball before me, and had taken my stance and adjusted my grip. Just as I was about to swing, a voice from behind me said, "Where are you aiming?" I turned and was met with a slight smile and the most piercing of clear blue eyes I had ever seen. That person was PGA Tour veteran Raymond Loran Floyd!

This assignment jettisoned from having the potential to be good, to being one of the best ever. The encounter was the first, but would not be the last time I would engage with Ray Floyd, and each time was a real privilege.

Our company had a contract with Mr. Floyd, and he was a great asset to our business. I learned a lot about golf from him, especially the need for precision regarding where you intend to hit the ball, and the need to actually visualize my shots before attempting to hit them.

These lessons helped me on the golf course for years to come. I regret, however, that I never told him how immeasurably what I had learned helped me throughout my career. I am certain that when most people hear the name Ray Floyd, they think of the great World Golf Hall of Fame member with 22 PGA Tour victories and four major championships. I think of that as well, however, I am most grateful for the unknowing mentor that he was to me.

I only had that position with the company for a brief six months, but it was among the most inspiring in my career because it also afforded me the opportunity to work with another golf legend who would later become the second woman inducted into the World Golf Hall of Fame and earn the distinction of receiving the PGA First Lady of Golf Award. That always "on," high-energy woman who was always a hit with our customers was Donna Caponi.

Donna's golf clinics were full of great golf tips, but she was especially adept in identifying what golf strengths an individual had – even if those strengths were only a kernel, as was the case with me!

She would offer specific instructions that immediately improved your game. She was a master at making you want to play better and making you believe you could. I love her obvious passion for the game and it inspired my own passion for golf, as well.

Building and Sustaining Relationships

As I look back at the years since my interest in golf was sparked, I am amazed by, and grateful for, the many ways in which the game has contributed to my enjoyment, my quality of life and the nuances of my leadership style. It has been one of the common denominators in many significant achievements.

As you may have noticed, relocation and changing jobs (always for the better, I am proud to say) has been one of the constants of my career. When you find another interested person, playing a round of golf with them is a really great way to really get to know the person, to explore issues of mutual interest and even talk about differences.

On more than one occasion, it was a golf outing that provided me the opportunity to spend quality time with fellow employees, key customers, elected officials and potential strategic partners to discuss economic growth, new product offerings, technological advancement and public policy issues. Truly, golf had also become a tool in my work.

Even for a very casual player like me, golf benefited me in some very surprising ways. For instance, I was deeply touched when a group of employees invited me to join them for a golf outing. Always looking for an opportunity to spend time with the many talented professionals who worked across the company, I readily accepted.

At the time, my older son, Aaron, had just finished his MBA program and was home interviewing with prospective employers. I saw this as a chance for him to meet, spend time with and get some advice and words of encouragement from a group of young professionals, so I invited him to come along. On the way home, he thanked me for including him and could not stop talking about what a great time he'd had. He mentioned the "great guys" he'd just met, the "real life" workplace situations and advice they had shared with him, and the much-appreciated words of encouragement extended to him.

It was just 10 days later that my son would die following major surgery. In the midst of my unbearable grief, I experienced a ray of sunshine, when the young men who had first met Aaron only days earlier, showed up at our home, dressed in dark suits and in cars that had been freshly washed and shined. They had come to honor Aaron and had volunteered to be "on call" to run errands, pick up family and guests from the airport and to simply be of assistance in any way they could. Some nine years later, this ranks as one of the most thoughtful expressions of kindness I have ever experienced. I am still comforted by the memory of their actions.

My husband, younger son, Evan, and I established The Aaron Ardoin Foundation for Sickle Cell Research and Education. The foundation raises funds to increase awareness, enhance treatment, promote prevention and advance the cure of sickle cell, the disease from which Aaron suffered and that contributed to his death.

The Inaugural Aaron Ardoin Foundation Golf tournament, sponsored by world Wide Technology and several other St. Louis businesses, was held October 2009 and was a huge fundraising success. Today, we look forward to supporting the mission of The Aaron Ardoin Foundation by partnering with other businesses to sponsor golf tournaments in communities across the United States to increase awareness and eventually cure this often-fatal disease. It is a testament to the role golf continues to play in supporting the many other charitable organizations today.

I am comforted beyond expression, when I reflect on the great time my son had that Saturday morning on the golf course and of the wonderful connections he made and the swell of confidence he gained at that course. Likewise, today I still reflect on the refrain of that Little Engine and say to myself, "I think I can, I think I can, I KNOW I CAN!"

About Priscilla Hill-Ardoin

Priscilla Hill-Ardoin is president of the PH-Agency, LLC, a consulting firm based in San Antonio, Texas and Founder of the Aaron Ardoin Foundation supporting sickle cell research and education. She is a seasoned senior executive with experience in corporate, civic, and public policy arenas. She began her management career in 1975 with Southwestern Bell Telephone, which later became SBC Communications and, ultimately, AT&T. During her tenure, she held numerous positions and worked on SBC's acquisition of Pacific Telesis, Ameritech, Bell South and AT&T. Hill-Ardoin was a pioneer at AT&T, having served as the company's first chief privacy officer, compliance officer and director of diversity. During her tenure, she established and managed AT&T's first enterprise-wide regulatory compliance organization and chaired the SBC Foundation.

Hill-Ardoin has become recognized for her generous charitable work and community service. She is the recipient of numerous awards, among them, the United Negro College Fund Excellence in Education Award, Voices for Children Super Hero Award, Girls Inc. Strong Smart and Bold Award, Congressional Black Caucus Women Opening the Pipeline Award, Purdue Distinguished Alumni award and a Washington University in St. Louis Distinguished Alumni Award. In 2005, she was inducted into the Minority Media and Telecom Council hall of Fame in Washington, D.C.

She currently serves as a director for Enterprise Holdings, Inc. She is also a Washington University trustee, a member of the Olin School of Business National Council and a director for Haven for Hope. Hill-Ardoin holds a bachelor's degree from Drury College, a master's degree from Purdue University, an MBA from Washington University, and a law degree from St. Louis University.

CHAPTER 27

Lessons Learned: No Reason to Wait Until You Are "Good Enough"

By Rita Turner

I will always remember that first, beautiful spring day that changed my life. I was at my desk, toiling over an earnings release and suddenly noticed that the sounds outside of my office were quite different from those on a typical afternoon. Typing had stopped. Phones were silent. Everything seemed very odd – especially the laughing and chattering going on among the secretaries.

I walked out of my office and asked, "What's going on?" My secretary, Rickie, responded, "Everyone's gone for the day." It was 11:30 in the morning! I followed with the obvious, "Why?" Rickie responded, "It's a beautiful day. They've all gone to play golf."

It was 1982, and I had recently been promoted to my first "executive" position at the bank. I was the "Executive Assistant" for Barney Taylor, chairman of Wilmington Trust Company. I was to learn the business, learn to think like a chairman and prepare myself for a senior management position. In Barney's words, I was to move up or move out.

At 28, I thought I knew it all, but I really knew very little. That spring day taught me my first lesson on succeeding in the male-dominated banking world. Looking at the women who served the administrative needs of the executive suite, I realized that I, too, was "one of the ladies" in the office. The executives were out on the golf course together, bonding over drives, putts and $5 Nassaus.

That day taught me that I had a choice: I could learn to play golf and be among the executives I wanted as my peers, or I could stay back at my desk and be seen as "one of the ladies" in the office pool. In a split second, I made the decision to take up golf.

That's how my life began to be shaped by the world of golf, and I owe much of my success in business and in life to this game. I even met my husband, Bob Grayson, through golf. So I hope my story will inspire you to give it a try or make it a greater part of your life.

My decision in 1982 was bigger than anticipated. Golf takes time – five or six hours, including travel – and I was busy with work and night school. It takes money – equipment and greens fees are expensive – and I was not earning an executive-level paycheck. It takes athletic talent – certainly eye/hand coordination, if nothing else – and I played no sports growing up. These were obstacles. But the BIG hurdle was adopting golf as part of the way I lived and worked.

I started with lessons from a professional. He was mechanical in his approach, and I developed a hitch in my swing just like the now-famous, often lampooned golf swing of former NBA star, Charles Barkley. Nonetheless, I shared my new conquest with my boss, who was thrilled, took me under his wing – and off to the driving range we went. He said I had "promise" and invited me to play with him and the bank's president, Sam.

We left the office the following week to play at Wilmington Country Club (Note: I was out of the office with the executives). I had never been on a golf course and it was beautiful, but I did not enjoy it. As soon as I stood over the ball, Barney told me what to do – every single time! I couldn't think, much less swing. Finally, Sam stepped in and said, "Rita, relax. It's just a game."

Undeterred, I stuck with it, going to the driving range and playing at public courses where I was paired with men I did not know. The guys didn't want to play with a woman, but inevitably, I would hit a good shot and the tension eased. Although difficult, these rounds were good – they got me out on the course where I actually played the game, rather than just hitting balls from a practice tee.

In 1990, I befriended Ginny, a fellow banker, who was a member at a country club. She invited me for nine holes after work and I was hooked! I joined Kennett Square Golf and Country Club the following week.

Then I ventured into business golf. By this time, I was chief marketing officer and had reasons to entertain and be entertained. I made it my business to know which clients were golfers and to find ways to invite them to play. Golf served two purposes: it got me out of the office like my male peers, and it gave me the means to connect with important contacts.

I extended my first invitation to a major client and included his loan officer. The client was a scratch golfer and the lender was almost as good, but I really didn't focus on that. Surprisingly, I played great and won a few holes with my 24 handicap before rain stopped us on the seventh hole. We drank scotch and told jokes for hours in the club grill after our round. It was a bonding experience and we are good friends, to this day.

Increasingly, golf became a big part of who I was and what I did, in business and in life. I grew to really love the game, and here are two reasons why. First, golf is a game about honesty and honesty is an important part of the game to be respected on the course. As golfers, we can call penalties on ourselves even if nobody sees the infraction. The rules of golf are self-enforced, which makes it unique as a game. I have met the nicest people I know through golf, which might be a reflection of the kind of people who are attracted to a sport like this.

The second reason I appreciate the game is because golf equalizes people. There is a handicap system in golf, but that's not to what I'm referring. In each round, every player is humbled by a bad shot and glorified by a remarkable shot at least once, no matter what the individual's skill level or social/professional position may be. In one round, I witness a senior vice president, who was a 12 handicap, score an 11 on a par four. Meanwhile, he saw me, a 27 handicap at the time, hit a shot within inches of making a hole-in-one. Of course, he also saw me miss many shots during that round, but there was something special about sharing both glory and humility alongside him that day.

So, I love this game! I have played it now for more than 30 years – something I never would have expected. I was reared in a household filled with music and dance as pastimes. My parents did not play golf or socialize with anyone who did. None of my siblings are golfers or interested in playing the game.

What happened to me? I think it was probably the combination of being in a male-dominated business and my personal ambition to succeed that drove me to golf. Whatever it was, I am eternally grateful for the advantages it has brought me.

Here are a few things I think have benefited me through playing this game:

Entering the Boy's Club: For a woman, golf connected me socially with my male colleagues. I was able to maneuver successfully in meetings, at lunch and during cocktail parties in their language. Understanding the meaning to the dialogue, such as, "I was laying three in the rough, got on the green and sank a ten footer for par," and how impressive it was on the par-five fourth hole at Merion Golf Club kept me in conversations – and credibly.

Building the Rolodex: By chance and great fortune, I met Chet, a master at using golf for business. Around 1994, a local club manager invited me to play the venerable Merion Golf Club, and Chet was our host member. After the round, Chet sent me a note and included a photo of us take on the course's eleventh tee, where a plaque commemorates the hole where Bobby Jones closed out the Grand Slam of his era with a win at the 1930 U.S. Amateur

Championship. This gesture made a lasting impression. And, I also made a friend for life who taught me the value of making connections through golf to expand my network.

Making an Impact: Golf does many good things, from raising money to teaching children strong values. I cherish the positive impacts I have made through my association with golf. For example, I was a founding advisory board member of the Urban Youth Golf Program, which introduced more than 2,500 Delaware kids to golf and its life lessons.

Making Mom Happy: Golf pushed me to do things. I played with some of the best golfers in the world, including LPGA Hall of Famer Betsy Rawls. I went to beautiful venues around the world. I teed it up while playing terribly – and came back to play again. Golf has made me a strong, confident person who can do anything she puts her mind to doing, as my mom always says.

I am a 17 handicap now. I can shoot 100 one day and 85 the next. Regardless, I can play with anyone as long as I play "respectable golf." This means hitting the ball somewhat consistently, knowing the rules, being pleasant to fellow golfers and adhering to proper golf etiquette. I also have rules that I live by when using golf for business.

- *Rule No. 1: Prepare Ahead of Time*. Take the time to know the details of the day. Are there locker facilities? Is there a dining facility? What are the directions to the course? I should know the answers to each of these questions before I go there to play.

- *Rule No. 2: Dress for the Occasion*. Stilettos and golf don't mix, but club dress codes can be less obvious. A female friend who arrived wearing a sleeveless, collarless shirt was embarrassed that her male host had to buy her a collared shirt to wear at his club. Don't risk a wardrobe malfunction on the course. Come prepared.

- *Rule No. 3: Arrive on Time*. It's easy to get sidetracked with things and leave a little late. Don't do it! As the host, arrive before your guests. As a guest, arrive at least 45 minutes before your tee time.

- *Rule No. 4: Be Responsible for Your Group.* Make sure your guests know the dress code and follow good golf etiquette. Forget your career round that day! Your job is to make sure the day goes well. Your guests will remember you fondly.

- *Rule No. 5: Nobody Cares About your Score.* If you think all eyes are on you, forget it. Hosting three men, I missed my first drive, scooting it 20 yards off the tee. When I got back in the cart my riding partner said, "Hit a good one?" He obviously was not watching – probably focused on HIS next shot.

- *Rule No. 6: Be Willing to Bomb.* Swing and swing again, with grace and humility. Your humanity is on public display. How you play at golf reflects how you play at business.

- *Rule no. 7: Make Getting there ALL the Fun.* It is all about how, not how many. The golfer who shoots 105 and was good company will forge much better relationships than the golfer who shoots 75 and was a pain in the neck that day.

I am not retired from banking, but golf is still a big part of my life. Bob and I enjoy playing golf together in Florida, where we now live. We have forged new friendships here through golf and stay in touch with our mid-Atlantic friends, many of whom we met through golf. People say golf is something you do your whole life. I would add that you cherish your golf friends and experiences forever.

For women reading this, I have one more story. It's about waiting to be perfect. I managed hundreds of people and was often sought out for mentoring. The first question I was often asked was, "How did you get where you are?" Answering that question with another question, I responded, "Where do you want to go?"

Most every woman will say she likes what she does, has much more to learn and eventually wants more when she is "ready." If SHE were a HE, he would say he wants my job or wants to be the chairman.

Women hold themselves back until they are "ready" – whatever "ready" means. I saw it in business and I say it in golf. Women were waiting until they were good enough before they would step out on the course. By comparison, no man ever turned me down for golf because he was not "good enough." And I've played with some very bad, male golfers.

The point is, now is the time to seize the opportunity. If you haven't ventured into golf, start now! If you have tried but haven't committed to be a player, commit now! And if you are already out on the links, play more! Opportunity awaits you.

About Rita Turner

Rita Turner is president and CEO of Rita Turner Enterprises, which she founded in 2011, specializing in competitive positioning for organizations in a global marketplace. Rita is a retired financial services executive who started her career at Wilmington Trust Company, Delaware, in 1973.

At Wilmington Trust, she held executive positions in marketing, strategic development, operations, risk management, compliance and administration. She served as chief marketing officer and chief operations officer and was the first female member of the firm's executive management committee, on which she served from 1996, until the firm's purchase by M&T Bank, New York, in May 2011. She led the integration of the two banks until her retirement, completing the integration in October 2011.

She has served on many boards, including as chairman of the board of the American Red Cross of the Delmarva Peninsula. She is a founder of the LPGA Urban Youth Golf Program in Wilmington, Del. (now a First tee program), a lifetime member of the N.A.A.C.P., and a member of the International women's forum.

Rita is passionate about advancing women in business. She has received numerous awards, including the 2010 discover girls, Inc. Award from U.S. Banker magazine; the inaugural "Rita Turner Award" from the YWCA Delaware in 2007; and the Jefferson Award from the United States Congress in 2002. She attended the University of Delaware and resides in Port St. Lucie, Fla.

CHAPTER 28

Promoting Golf As A "Team Sport" In Mexico

By Rosalba Papacostas and Marina Villasana

As Mexicans, we are proud of our country and of all that was accomplished in golf by former LPGA star Lorena Ochoa, but we also recognize the challenges for Mexican women to follow in Lorena's footsteps.

After meeting many young Mexican women and girl golfers, we wanted to ensure that those who are competitive enough could reach their dream of playing professional golf in the United States. We wanted them to have opportunities that our generation did not have.

That's why we decided to take advantage of the momentum that Lorena created in our home nation. In 2008, we launched our effort as Impulsando al Golf Professional Mexicano (IGPM), a non-profit association established to create a team philosophy among aspiring Mexican professional golfers.

Sports are big in Mexico, but most of the focus is on soccer and boxing. These sports also get most of the media's attention. The opportunity for ordinary people to play golf is still limited and the development of a golf infrastructure is in its early stages in our country.

There was no sports media coverage here of a young girl who was breaking every record in junior golf on a world level. As a Mexican junior, Lorena Ochoa had one of the brightest records in amateur golf in the history of U.S. Golf Association championships, as well as at the NCAA Division I Women's Golf Championship while she was a student at the University of Arizona. She also won five straight Junior World Championships – a record not even Tiger Woods achieved.

When Lorena turned professional, she continued to win and it was only then that Mexico discovered what we had. She was becoming the greatest athlete ever born in this country. When her stellar career was over, she was not only a future LPGA Hall of Fame candidate, but also a source of pride and inspiration for Mexican boys and girls just taking up golf.

While inspirational, Lorena's story was really atypical. Her fast rise to the top of women's golf had not made us aware that, for most players, such a journey is long and difficult and requires continued support for many years – especially in the early stages of a young professional's career.

The second Mexican woman to earn her LPGA Tour card was Violeta Retamoza, an All-American at the University of Tennessee. Violeta's path to the LPGA was also fast, but she soon realized that Mexicans needed a solid structure to transition from a successful amateur career to a spot alongside the LPGA's best players.

One of the main challenges for that transition is that amateur players usually belong to a club, state team, or national or university team. These institutions often cover financial needs and offer a support system allowing the player to focus only on their day-to-day performance in golf. Those players benefit from *team* support.

We learned that most Mexican women golfers felt alone when they turned professional because they lacked that team of supporters. Some turned professional only to realize their talent was not enough to help them succeed on the professional level. After her first LPGA season, Violeta shared her story with us and the stories of many other golfers chasing their dreams in the U.S. on the professional tours.

She described how she was "amazed to meet people who had such enthusiasm" to help her peers. Violeta told us: "I knew a huge change was coming for women's golf in Mexico and that I was going to have an opportunity to be part of it."

We learned these young women were traveling throughout the U.S. with very limited resources, driving great distances on their own with no support other than from family and friends. Some had turned their cars into their homes with the back seat serving as a closet. They found it difficult to perform at the highest level when they could not afford hotels. The nomadic lifestyle as touring professionals in another country, moving to a new city or state each week, took adjustment.

And yet, these were talented women with the passion and the discipline required to succeed in the game. As their friends, we wondered how could we help? How could we attract the interest of potential sponsors, of media and sports authorities to create awareness of the challenges these aspiring pros faced? How could we turn it into a new platform for the development of talented young women who dream of becoming a world-class players?

We started our non-profit association to create a team to assist these aspiring Mexican professional golfers. Since the launch of our project five years ago, many have joined our effort and now Violeta, retired from competitive golf, volunteers as part of IGPM to help communicate with the professional players. This has provided continuous dialogue with the golfers we support and has given us a better understanding of their needs.

We were just concerned individuals who had no connection to professional golf and no daughters involved in the sport. Our efforts were intially received with some skepticism, but ultimately, the objective nature of our intent helped the credibility of our effort. We had no personal stakes, no profit involved and no blood relatives who would benefit from the program. All we had when we started IGPM was our love for the game and the aim to set an example of teamwork that could inspire other sports institutions in our country.

Soon, others embraced this concept. They too, wanted opportunity for our young pros and wanted to help them succeed. Those who got involved with IGPM offered essential leadership. They have been more than sponsors; they have encouraged us, shared advice and helped us network.

This effort grew from women promoting a non-profit sports group to suddenly working side by side with some of our nation's top "movers and shakers" – such as: Carlos Bremer, one of the most prominent businessmen and promoters of sports in our comunity; Luis Carlos Villarreal, a talented businessman who shares our passion for golf; Eugenio Azcarraga and Miguel Ruiz, top executives of Televisa, Mexico's leading TV and media company; and Renato Sandoval, a young entrepreneur and owner of *Golf and Spa Magazine*, Mexico's top golf magazine.

But even with solid private sponsors, getting our goverment to join and support the project remained a challenge. Golf had been considered an elite sport and authorities were reluctant to allocate resources in a way that was relevant for female professional golfers. But finally, with the support of the Mexican Golf Federation, we offered a new way to combine efforts.

What started as an isolated contribution has turned into an institutionalized program by the National Sports Comission (CONADE) to provide benefits to IGPM. Leaders at CONADE joined IGPM and became a key pillar for our association. One of our purposes was to transform the image of golf as an individual sport and to build the concept of a national team effort.

Our annual pro-am tournament, also started in 2008, is used to increase awareness and raise funds for our association. This event brings together players, sponsors, golf authorities, organizers, volunteers and supporting fans. Lorena Ochoa and her coach Rafael Alarcon, have been present in every one of our pro-ams, showing their unconditional support for our efforts. One of the most respected and experienced golfers in Mexico, Rafael has always been available to provide advice and guidance for IGPM .

Top Mexican men professional golfers also have traveled from many different places to show their solidarity and to contribute to the success of our pro-am fund-raising efforts. Their participation and interest is a testimony of the highest level of sportmanship and camaraderie.

In addition, top LPGA Tour members have participated in our pro-ams to support their Mexican friends. Although they all compete against each other on the LPGA Tour, the players are friends and are willing to give their time so funds may be raised to support their fellow competitors. The positive energy created by having other players support our golfers, for no personal benefit, is a priceless reward for our time and effort.

This combination of efforts is the underlying philosophy of IGPM and it has allowed our association to grow. IGPM first started providing support for two players, and now, the program has grown to support many more players.

IGPM still does not cover all of their needs, but as players who compete against each other individually, they must learn to work as a team, share experiences and to encourage each other. They all wear our logo on their clothing. Yes, they compete as individuals, but they also are a team.

Mexican professionals Lili Alvarez, Tanya Dergal, Devan Andersen, Sophia Sheridan and Marcela Leon were the first players that inspired the creation of IGPM. After them, Pamela Ontiveros, Ale Llaneza and Margarita Ramos have joined our team. We hope others will follow.

We have helped our players understand this is not only about receiving financial support, but it's also an effort that requires their time, commitment and sharing of experiences with younger players following in their path. Our dream is to have many more successful Mexican golfers. To get there, we must continue building a sense of community among our players, sponsors and golf authorities.

Although IGPM has been able to provide some financial help to our players, we believe that our main accomplishment has been to involve many others in this effort. There is much more to be done, as we are not yet providing a complete program for aspiring golfers, but such a goal will only be achieved if more companies and institutions join this initiative.

This program was dreamed up by amateur women golfers in a nation not previously known for golf success, but from our perspective, IGPM is everyone's project. What has been accomplished, and all that can still be achieved, will be the result of a collaborative effort. We are proud of our results and we hope others can feel ownership of what we have built together.

We also hope that we are now building a model for the future to develop young talent in Mexico. Individuals really can make a difference and we hope what we have created is a trail that can be followed by future generations of golfers in our country.

About Rosalba Papacostas de Gutierrez and Marina Jones de Villasana

Rosalba was born in Tampico, Mexico, and was the youngest of a family of four sisters and one brother. As a child, she participated in many sports, such as swimming, volleyball and tennis. She played college tennis and softball at Monterrey Tech.

After obtaining a degree in marketing, she started and ran her own company until she took time to rear a family. Marrying an avid golfer, Rosalba took up golf at 27 and soon held a 13 handicap.

At her club in Monterrey, Mexico, she was head of Las Misiones Country Club's Junior Golf Committee for several years, encouraging participation by boys and girls. Her three children, all involved in sports, are: Pablo, 18, Isabel, 16, and David, 10.

Rosalba also practices yoga, Zhineng Qigong, meditation and enjoys nature activities. She is co-founder and current president of IGPM.

Marina was born in Monterrey Mexico, the eldest of three brothers and sisters. She played numerous youth sports, including bowling and softball. She earned a degree in communications from the University of Monterrey and worked for the Mexican Educational System for many years after graduating.

Marina currently plays golf to a 12 handicap, and also volunteers with various golf institutions in Mexico. She has served as president of Mexico's Northern Region Junior Golf Committee. She was vice president of the Mexican Women's Golf Association. She is currently vice president of the Mexican Association of Northern Golf Clubs.

Marina is married and has five children and five grandchildren. She is co-founder and vice president of IGPM.

CHAPTER 29

Seeing the Game of Golf Through A Woman's Eyes

By Thadine Clifton

The day was like any other day at the annual PGA Merchandise Show in Orlando, Fla., where more than 1,000 golf companies and brands welcome thousands of PGA Professionals and golf shop buyers from over 75 countries to see the latest in golf equipment, products, services and apparel. With more than 40,000 in attendance, there was optimism for a strong year in the golf business. But this year, instead of parking myself in a trade-show booth with my product, I decided to see the show through a different set of eyes.

So I made my way to the show's Demo Day which featured equipment manufacturers demonstrating their latest products at a local golf club just a short distance from the Orange County Convention Center.

Why was I there? As president of my company, Collé Products, I wanted to see firsthand how my new club cleaning product, Golf Shine, could make a difference to consumers playing the game with clean shiny clubs! Upon arrival, I was certainly in the minority but ready to learn and make my mark. Remember, thousands of PGA (male) professionals make the pilgrimage to Orlando each January.

That is where I met Chris Mass, the director of client resources for the National Golf Foundation. We spent the day viewing and testing the trade show products and sharing our perspectives on the golf business.

When I mentioned writing a chapter in a golf book, Chris said he "immediately thought of another beautiful and outspoken woman in golf, LPGA Tour veteran Jan Stephenson." Chris said Jan always portrayed herself as a *woman* first, bringing her unique views and style to the game.

He noted that Jan's opinion was women in golf should be confident, strong and attractive and sell that persona to golf fans, as well as fellow male and female players. Chris added: "She reminds me of you, Thadine."

I took note of Chris and his comments and thought about the development of my own business and my relationship with the game and how it evolved.

I am often at high-profile events and exhibitions and have a keen eye for spotting new trends. My first product "Shine," an eco-friendly jewelry cleaner, was developed because of an experience I had at an event where I was getting a manicure and noticed my ring needed cleaning. When I asked the manicurist if she had a cleaning solution at the nail salon and she didn't, the idea hit me. It was my "aha" moment! I knew as the owner of a chemical company, I could figure out an eco-friendly solution to do-it-yourself, on-the-go jewelry cleaning. That is how "Shine" was born. At that time, I had no idea that Shine would have a golf application and both products would have a tremendous market niche."

As for my own course preferences, I admire women who love playing 18 holes of golf. As a woman running two companies, I very rarely have the 4-5 hours needed to play 18 holes. The solution I found was The Society of Nine Holes. I'm truly a "Nine Holer." Nine holes of golf is the perfect time format for a working mother, busy women professionals and other women who work their schedules around their families' needs.

My true heart's desire was to be a television sportscaster at a time when women did not exist in that realm. You see, I am one of six children. I have always been athletic. Being raised at the shore provided an environment for the most exhilarating sports. I loved surfing, water skiing, sailing, skateboarding, playing tennis and even skiing in the dead of winter. Each sport had its unique seasonal attributes.

As a child, I attended a Catholic high school that had no funds for sports. Having no sports in school was the driving force for me to convince my parents to allow me to attend public school, so off to public school I went!

To my amazement, the first time a golf club – an iron – was placed in my hands was during a physical education class. My gym teacher was so astonished that I whacked the ball like a line drive. I was naturally gifted with strong legs and was incredibly comfortable playing golf.

So my love of golf began. It began at a time when my dad belonged to a country club. He played on the weekends and once during the week. No, he wasn't a doctor. He was a lawyer. And in those days, no women graced the country club or the golf course.

It wasn't until years later when these members' second wives came along – who were much younger – that women began infiltrating the country club. They played golf and took lessons while their husbands worked.

Fast forward, and I am now in the workforce. Although I worked in sports public relations, I did not become the broadcaster I desired to be. I worked in the chemical industry which truly was a man's world.

The German chemical company I worked for, with its European influence, was exceptional. As a company, we played volleyball, tennis and went skiing together. I began in an entry-level position, was trained at the World Trade Center and promoted into marketing.

However, I noticed that the male salesmen were treated like royalty – much like the pharmaceutical salesmen and the Wall Street guys. I coveted that position. I struck out on my own to obtain the sales position my heart yearned for.

As my sales career evolved, it came to my attention that everyone was doing business on the golf course. My boss was great, yet the old adage of "the good old boys club" still rang true. I soon learned that if you want to play with the big boys, you have to know how to play golf, so I began focusing on becoming proficient in this game.

Originally, I had no desire to play golf recreationally, but once I did, I found that I had so much fun. I also found that being among the most comforting, calming, peaceful, relaxing, breathtaking landscapes brings an enlightened dimension to both business dealings and my personal life.

Fast forward once again, and I invented, branded, promoted and launched two consumer products. One is a golf-consumer lifestyle product that is simple, classy and elegant, like the game itself.

I believe golf is a lifestyle, not just a game. That is when I went back to golf in my own way. I noticed that Ralph Lauren Polo was designing women's golf apparel. That's when it hit me – when you dress the part, you play the part, and you enjoy a better game. You are confident.

Yes, attractive, sporty outfits are part of the expensive repertoire. I purchased the most luxurious Italian women's golf wear I could find. Talk about life changing! My professional contacts climbed the ladder to the higher echelon. I also began playing at the top clubs in the Northeast.

While playing golf, I have forged and bonded in various professional relationships. Company outings provide sponsorships that bring people to an elevated level of camaraderie. I play seriously, competitively, and have the utmost respect for the game. This dynamic allows me to play on a more accomplished player's level. This in turn gained my colleagues' respect.

But it is not all about business. Golf has brought me the comfort of tradition, yet the synergistic growth of the sport. It brings back old memories that light up my smile and at the same time, progressively moves us into the future. The game surrounds us with individuals who are positive, uplifting, health conscious and who love the outdoor sociality of the game.

I feel that the game of golf embraces life's essence. It gives us the beauty of the outdoors, the social connections, relationship-building skills and the ability to achieve personal greatness. To bring these elements into the lives of others gives me great joy. I gave each of my high school babysitters and my own daughters the gift of golf lessons when they graduated from high school. I told them go to college and to learn all they could, but to also learn more about golf, and then come out swinging into the business world.

Today, golf has morphed into a family-bonding experience. It is no longer considered only a "man's game." It's a blessing to see women on the golf course. We now see those women's children and their children's children effortlessly walking the course and playing the game.

Gratefully, today's women have shattered the country club's glass ceiling. And those beautiful women are confident, strong women, who also love this amazing game of golf.

About Thadine Clifton

With 25 years of experience in specialty chemical cleansers, customer service, and waste management, Thadine Clifton, president and CEO at Collé Corporation and Collé Products built two successful, certified, female-owned and operated businesses.

A resident of Mountain Lakes, N.J., and a mother of two, Thadine has prided herself on her eco-conscious focus and entrepreneurial skills. Her new company Collé Products, established in January 2010, launched its first product, Shine – a luxury jewelry-cleaning mousse, from the Collé Collection.

Just as she did in the industrial-cleaning business, eco-conscious Thadine created a foray into the jewelry arena to protect the earth from harsh and harmful chemicals. Shine by Collé is the first in the line of new, nontoxic consumer products designed for those who want to look their best, while remaining environmentally conscious. The success of Shine led Thadine to her new product showcase at the 2010 Oscars in Los Angeles, as well as at the 2010 Gift Guide Media Show in New York City.

Additionally, Thadine co-chairs the Annual United Nations weekend, a 48-year-old tradition within the United Nations Secretariat, as well as One to World, formerly Metro International. A percentage of proceeds along with product from Collé Collections get donated to many charitable organizations.

CHAPTER 30

Golf As The Constant Through Life's Ups and Downs

By Tyra Jarvis

My relationship with golf began more than 40 years ago. Throughout the years, the game has been there for me – in good times and in the not-so-good times. It has been a constant wherever I lived, worked and played.

In the beginning, golf competed for my time and attention among many other sports and activities. My relationship with golf was recreational; we were "just friends." Today, golf is my sport of choice and my single sports focus. Our relationship is exclusive and I am an avid golfer.

Currently a 14 handicap, I strive to: play at least 52 rounds each year; someday earn a single-digit handicap; and experience a hole-in-one! I take lessons regularly to improve my game, compete inside and outside EWGA events, and play with my family and friends for fun. I also follow the LPGA and PGA Tours.

Golf introduced me to the EWGA, where I gained nonprofit business experience and leadership development opportunities not afforded to me elsewhere in my career. The game has helped me build strong interpersonal relationships with my friends and colleagues at work, enhance my leadership and management skills, and cultivate a robust resource network of contacts instrumental in developing my Kefi Coaching practice. I chose coaching as the next step in my career because I love working with intelligent, passionate individuals and teams, supporting them in impacting results and fulfilling their dreams to realize their full potential.

Golf was there for me during my husband Jim's courageous battle with melanoma and continues to be, as I navigate my grieving process since his passing. Occasional golf outings with girlfriends provided brief and needed reprieves from my role as caregiver. Golf is a constant reminder – albeit bittersweet – of my life with Jim and the big role it played in our relationship.

Whenever I play golf, I feel close to Jim. It's sad to reminisce the times gone by and the future that will never be. At the same time, I believe really feeling and expressing the emotions of loss and grief is the only way to move forward – just like golf, one shot at a time.

My process included pushing myself to walk onto the course as a single for the first time. It was also memorable when I scattered some of Jim's ashes on the 18th fairway of the K Club on an EWGA trip to Ireland. The rain poured that day, but when we reached the 18th hole, the clouds parted and the sun appeared.

My dad introduced me to golf while I was in high school. Back then, girls were not allowed to wear pants to school, physical education was required for all four years, and there was no Title IX. I was very athletic, excelled in P.E., and lettered in gymnastics for four years.

My dad was a golf fanatic. Any time he was not at work, he was at our neighborhood municipal golf course. Always known as a flashy dresser, golf provided a safe place for him to wear vibrant color-coordinated outfits in pink, turquoise and peach with matching hats.

The local club professional, Roly Lamontagne, came from the Boston area where we were from, and he and my dad became lifelong friends. One day, my sisters and I were invited to the practice tee for our first lesson with Roly. Dad had focused so much attention on my brother's game, and now it was our turn. My dad and Roly were excited to share the game they both loved with us.

Fortunately, my first on-course lesson was with my dad. I remember walking to the putting green and pulling out my driver – my favorite club and the only one I hit very well. He looked at me with a quizzical expression on his face. That's when I learned from him that my putter was the appropriate club.

Roly continued to play a role in my early years with golf. My first husband worked for him at another local golf course. By now, I had my own clubs. We would play any chance we could. I never broke 100, and I didn't worry much about the rules but I loved being outside, walking the course and hitting the ball. Perhaps if I knew then, what I know now, I may have thought I didn't play well enough to join a group, an outing or an event, but I was *always* ready to play.

I entered the workforce right out of high school. Even though I was college prep and accepted at Sacramento State University, I was expected to go to work and begin supporting myself. My mom worked for the telephone company and helped me get my first job as a telephone operator.

It wasn't long before I wondered, "Is this all there is?" So, I began the quest to earn a promotion into management. I started going to college while I worked full time with the goal to qualify for the company's "Obtained Degree While Employed" (ODWE) program. I also took advantage of the upgrade and transfer program to gain experience with different areas of the business.

One of those opportunities was in outside plant construction as a cable maintenance splicer. This was a way to obtain field experience to become more promotable. It was also a way to earn substantially more money.

This was during the 1970s' "Women's Movement" and women in outside plant work were still relatively new. I took this job assignment very seriously. It was not the most hospitable of environments for women and I felt constantly under pressure to prove myself. This was a physically and emotionally tough assignment and I learned a lot about myself. Most significantly, I learned there was nothing I *couldn't* do – only things I didn't like to do. Nobody, including the guys, liked climbing a rotten telephone pole in 40 mph winds! Once I realized that, I didn't feel constantly tested to prove myself.

Many of the guys also played golf and would take off days to play together. I was always invited. I loved being able to spend time with these guys away from the pressures of work. They too, were more relaxed and we had a great time. It made being with them at work a lot easier. It also helped me to be accepted as "one of the guys" and it made me more comfortable playing golf with male co-workers in any setting.

One of my most memorable golf outings was when our co-worker checked us in and we were called to the first tee as "Mitchell, Haldeman, Ehrlichman and Nixon" – key figures in the infamous Watergate scandal. We all looked at each other and cracked up.

I earned my bachelor's degree and became the first member of my family to graduate from something other than the "College of Hard Knocks!" Successful in the company's ODWE program, I was transferred to Pacific Bell Yellow Pages and relocated to the San Francisco Bay area. It was a wonderful new opportunity, but I was away from my family and friends for the first time. So, I joined an employee golf club, the PacTel Par Chasers – a coed golf group of mostly men – where I began my more serious relationship with golf.

The club offered organized monthly play and a few weekend getaways. I established a handicap for the first time and began taking regular lessons. My co-workers also played golf and I was invited to play with them. We took annual golf trips and I joined a team to play in the annual AT&T fundraiser.

During this time, I began dating my dear friend Jim, who would later become my second husband. Jim was an avid golfer. He joined the Par Chasers and we joined a private club. This was not an easy decision for me. A few years earlier, I had been asked on the eighth green to leave a private course because it was "Men's Day!" Fortunately, we found Auburn Valley Country Club, a progressive, gender-neutral club in our area, with equal access to tee times and facilities for all members.

We played golf at Cypress Point. We even took a week of vacation in the Sacramento area to volunteer at an LPGA tournament – the Longs Drugs Challenge. The course was also the host club for the local EWGA Chapter. Jim spotted an EWGA membership brochure in the pro shop and handed it to me.

Little did I know how my relationship with golf and the EWGA would impact my life, both personally and professionally. I joined the EWGA that week and was playing with the group by the following weekend. This was exactly what I was looking for – a way to improve my game, play more golf with women and to reestablish my network in the Sacramento area. At our events, there were box lunches, raffle prizes, destinations, conferences, spas and great new friends. The friends I have met through the EWGA are still my closest girlfriends.

I was initially attracted to the EWGA for its nationwide network of working women, its unique emphasis on golf as a critical business skill and the organization's role in advocating issues of importance to women golfers. I later became an EWGA volunteer. Hooked on the EWGA's volunteer leadership opportunities and experiences, I moved quickly through the volunteer leadership ranks.

Working with a non-profit organization is a great way to learn and practice leadership and business skills. Serving on the EWGA's Board of Directors was an incredible experience. My efforts were valued and appreciated as I made a difference for our members, our volunteers and in the golf community.

Some may say I'm a self-made female executive. I have taken advantage of every opportunity available to advance my career, including playing golf, which has been there every step of my way. I had golf when I transitioned from blue collar to white collar; when I moved from Sacramento to the Bay Area and back; from being a corporate team player and leader to a business owner; and now, as I move forward in my grieving process.

Golf has offered a resource network of quality contacts who have supported me as I develop and grow my coaching practice, as well as providing my most memorable life experiences. It is a game shared with members of my family, among my closest girlfriends and with my teams at work. It is definitely a game for life – my life.

About Tyra Jarvis

Tyra Jarvis is founder and president of Kefi Coaching LLC, a personal and professional coaching practice. Her areas of focus are career and life transition, leadership development and business and executive coaching. A proven leader, she partners with clients in a process of listening, discovery, problem solving, action planning and accountability that values empowerment and individual responsibility to support her clients in translating their passion and goals into reality.

Her professional experience is built upon a 30-plus-year career in the "hypercompetitive" telecommunications industry, planning and implementing enterprise-wide technology and business projects. She specializes in translating creative, innovative ideas into practical action, ensuring successful execution and making a difference for individuals and organizations, both profit and not-for-profit.

Tyra also served on the EWGA Board of Directors, where she led the board in its first in-depth strategic planning process resulting in its first five-year strategic plan. This plan drove the development and implementation of a strategy to expand and restructure the EWGA Board, adding critical skills and expertise, along with increased member, golf industry and corporate representation. This restructuring improved the EWGA's volunteer leadership structure at the governance level, as well as strengthened and stabilized its management.

Reared in Boston and Sacramento, Calif., Tyra holds a bachelor's degree in organizational behavior and environment from California State University-Sacramento and an MBA in telecommunications from the University of San Francisco, earning both degrees while working full time. She currently resides in Auburn, Calif., where she enjoys playing golf. Vacations not involving golf are the exception, not the rule.

ENRICHING LIVES

Each year, the EWGA Foundation awards its Women On Par® Scholarship to provide financial assistance to "non-traditional" female students. The scholarship is intended for women, age 30 and older, who are attending a college or university for the first time or returning to school after an absence to complete their technical/vocational, associate or bachelor's degree.

The scholarship is designed to help these women get "on par" or achieve equal footing with their peers, friends or other women who have had a chance to complete their college education.

The EWGA Foundation Women On Par® Scholarship was established in 2007, with the first scholarship awarded in 2008. To date, 10 scholarships have been awarded since the program started. One scholarship for $1,000 and one for $500 is awarded each year.

Marilyn Bunag of San Francisco was the 2010 EWGA Foundation Women On Par® Scholarship recipient. Bunag recently graduated with honors with a 3.96 grade-point average and earned her bachelor's degree in sociology at San Francisco State University.

A single mother of four, Bunag first earned her associate degree at City College of San Francisco and then her bachelor's degree while working and rearing her family. She is now a program manager at Arriba Juntos (Upward Together), a nonprofit agency that provides tools for women challenged by domestic abuse, drug addiction and poverty and empowers them to get on their feet, earn degrees and join the workforce.

Bunag's personal story follows in the next chapter as she describes how she escaped her own life of poverty, drug addiction and domestic abuse. She plans to start graduate school next spring and is determined to set a solid example for her children.

In correspondence with the EWGA as she progressed through her undergraduate studies, Bunag referenced a quote by comedian Milton Berle that said: "If opportunity doesn't knock, build a door."

"We are a family of women all about empowering other women and helping them to succeed," said EWGA CEO Pam Swensen. "EWGA helped Marilyn build that door."

CHAPTER 31

If Opportunity Doesn't Come Knocking, Build a Door
By Marilyn Bunag

Sometimes the women in our program at Arriba Juntos (Upward Together) look at me in disbelief when I tell them they can escape things in their lives that prevent them from living fully. Sometimes their jaws drop when I tell them I have been "clean" from drug abuse for 11 years.

They look at me as if to say, "You? You struggled with these things?" And I look at them in their eyes and tell them I truly understand how they feel because I *have* been there. I assure them there is support to help them and I challenge them to get busy making a difference in their own lives.

Maybe I was one of the lucky ones. Lucky that I wanted more in my life and better lives for my children. Lucky that I made up my mind to get out of poverty. Lucky that I believed there was more for me than addiction to methamphetamines or that I didn't have to believe my ex-husband when he would strike me and tell me I was "worthless" and a "bad mother."

I spent many years living in the cycle of poverty in which I was reared. I grew up with some of the same issues my mother had. She brought me to the

United States from the Philippines when I was 2. She had a sixth-grade education and basic English skills. She worked at fast-food restaurants and in housekeeping, doing the best she could do with no skills and no educational degrees.

When I was 10, my five younger siblings became my responsibility as my mother developed a crippling gambling addiction and a problem with alcohol. Years passed and I found myself grappling with the things I disliked the most about my upbringing. In a blink of an eye, I looked into a mirror one day and saw my mother's image: I was a 37-year-old single mother raising four children of my own; I was a former drug addict; and I was a survivor of incredible domestic violence.

I think the turning point for me to change my life literally came at the barrel of a gun. My ex-husband put a gun to my face. I shut my eyes. I thought, "This is it." In that instant, I thought about my kids. I thought about my life. I didn't want to die. I thought, "I'm worth more than this." As scary as it was, it was my wake-up call.

He went to jail for drugs and I knew that was my opportunity to escape. I got a restraining order, knowing he would eventually get out, and then I went into treatment to escape my addiction to methamphetamines. My mother saw what was happening and encouraged me to get help. I think she thought I would either be killed or imprisoned for the drugs and she realized that our family had to do something to help ourselves. She said she would help with my kids while I got treatment.

Around that same time, I learned that I was pregnant with my fourth child, Matthew. I had to get off the drugs for him and that pregnancy made me realize this was the time to do it. This was the time I needed to think about my family. Matthew saved my life.

I stayed in treatment for eight months. There, I had support and counseling and I could talk about my own demons. I could understand them better and learn what to do to break this cycle of addiction. Being away from my family for those months was really difficult, but it was something I needed to do.

Once I got through the treatment, I was able to get transitional housing – an apartment – and I could bring my children. We lived there for three years and I worked in an office. There was a support staff and a therapist available where we lived if I needed it, but I was slowly getting stronger and more confident. They encouraged me to go to school, so I started classes at City College of San Francisco.

In 2008, I earned my associate degree with highest honors. With my family and children in the audience cheering me on, walking onstage to receive my diploma was an overwhelming rite of passage. I had no example for education in my family, but I am proud to say I created that precedent.

It wasn't easy at all, but I had a goal. I knew the only way out of poverty and to be an inspiration to my kids was through education. I had many fears, but I had teachers who believed in me. I started getting A's and I liked it. All my life, I had felt worthless, but when I got "clean," I started seeing the world differently. People believed in me and that helped me to believe in myself.

Still, a four-year college degree seemed so far away. I was talking to one of the teachers at the junior college one day about getting my bachelor's degree and I said, "I'll be 40 years old. That's old to still be in college." But she said, "You're going to be 40 anyway, so why not be 40 with a bachelor's degree?"

So, I dedicated myself to finishing my bachelor's degree. I enrolled at San Francisco State University and continued working while going to college. My kids and I did homework together at night. When I got a good grade, I'd say, "Look, I got an A," and then my kids would show me their A's and we had fun comparing our grades.

There were a lot of long nights for me. I would study until 2 a.m., and then get up for work at 6 a.m. They sacrificed a lot, too. Sometimes I would say, "Sorry, we can't go there because I have a paper due." And then I reminded them I was doing this for our future so they could have a better life together.

I graduated magna cum laude in May 2012 with a degree in health and human sciences and was selected by the dean and department chairs of my college to receive the symbolic investiture of the hood on behalf of my fellow students at commencement. Six of us were honored at the top of our respective colleges of study from among 8,000 graduates at San Francisco State.

It was awesome to share that with my family and they were proud of me. I wanted to show my children that education is the key and that college is a real possibility. I've heard that if a parent has a bachelor's degree, their children are more likely to earn their college degrees, as well.

I became a case manager at Arriba Juntos after I earned my associate degree. They promoted me to programs manager when I earned my undergraduate degree in 2012. Now, my goal is to start graduate school in Spring 2014 to earn my master's degree in public administration.

But none of this would have been possible if others had not believed in me. Teachers, therapists and even the EWGA Foundation that awarded me the Women On Par® Scholarship believed in me and they didn't even know me. I learned about it by searching on the Internet for scholarship opportunities for non-traditional women. And I was that – a low-income, adult woman looking for assistance.

I worried that I had to be a golfer to get a scholarship, but fortunately, that was not in the criteria. Still, every time I see golf on TV, I think about those women of the EWGA who love golf and made this opportunity available to me. I am so grateful because I know it doesn't always work out like this for women from backgrounds like mine.

I have traveled down roads that led to nowhere, but I'm proof that it is never too late to change the direction of your life. I have been granted a second chance and I am making the most of it. I am a woman making productive, positive choices in life.

My college diploma hangs on the wall and it's the first thing I see when I step into the house. It seems surreal, sometimes. Amazing, all the time – a symbol of a lot of hard work and proof that hard work renders rewards.

Now, I work with women who were just like me. I think my life experiences totally shape the way I can help other people. I understand. *I really do*. Like many of them, I have also been on welfare, food stamps and I've struggled with transportation issues and childcare as a single mom.

In my past life as an addict, I made some bad decisions. I wasn't always there for my children. Today, I'm open and honest with my kids and I tell them drugs ruin lives. I tell them I wasn't there for them because of the drugs. The good thing is, they forgave me, and I'm here now – 120 percent.

I guess it took hitting rock bottom for me to realize I needed help. I had to learn a lot of things the hard way, but at least I learned them. I knew I could do better, but I just needed to get all the negative aspects out of my life. I knew I could shine, but I needed support and self-esteem.

I knew I didn't want to be beaten up by my husband, but I stayed with him because I didn't know there were resources out there for me or places for me to go with my children to be safe. Now, I can tell other women where to go for help and I can tell them they are not alone.

I saw a quote on the Internet once from comedian Milton Berle that said, "If opportunity doesn't knock, build a door." Some people do have barriers in life when it comes to opportunity and maybe their path is not as easy as it is for some, but I can honestly say that anyone can find a way to build their own door to reach goals. You have to set goals and work toward them. And most of all, you can never give up.

About Marilyn Bunag

Marilyn graduated Magna Cum Laude in May 2012 from San Francisco State University with a bachelors of arts degree in Sociology. Following graduation, she landed a job at Arriba Junta and was shortly thereafter promoted to her present position as Program Manager.

As a program manager, Marilyn currently supervises six staff members and is responsible for providing English classes, computer classes and the tools and skills to program participants to help them join the workforce. She plans to study public administration in graduate school in Spring 2014.

Marilyn is the mother of four children and says her goal is to see her children graduate from college.

EPILOGUE

Book's Contributing Authors Are Reminders Of Why We Play Golf

By Lisa D. Mickey

I didn't really know what to expect when I was asked to edit the chapters written by career women for the EWGA's "Teeing Up For Success" book project. For the last 20-plus years, I have worked in the golf industry and my view of the game has been fixed from a level that most people don't experience.

In a way, writing and thinking about golf every day ruined it for me on a personal level. I rarely play anymore. I rarely *want* to play. Leisure time is now spent on a bicycle or in a kayak.

I still love golf, but part of the reason I'm taking a timeout from playing is that I used to work for a large national golf magazine where golf prowess was scrutinized. I had a golf handicap of 6 when I went there to work. I enjoyed playing new and challenging courses and when my male colleagues said, "Let's go play golf," off I went.

There was just one problem – they always wanted to play for money. I was very uncomfortable putting my hard-earned cash on my golf game on difficult golf courses, but that's the only way my colleagues played the game. I sweated out every cent on every putt. And my joy in the game began slipping away.

Each year, our company held an in-house tournament called "The Editor's Putter" and all of the editors and writers would spend a day playing a company-wide, match-play event on a tough golf course. One year, we all traveled to Far Hills, N.J., home to the United States Golf Association. We played our tournament on a course near the USGA's headquarters and one of their former championship directors set up the course for our company event.

I don't have much experience in match play other than covering it as a writer at the U.S. Women's Amateur Championship or the Solheim Cup, so I had no idea how I would play in this format. One thing that comforted me was this golf course's greens were super fast – like, 13 on a Stimpmeter! It was like putting on a very slick linoleum floor. But I love bentgrass greens, and in particular, I love fast, true greens that allow a ball to track right into the cup.

I won the tournament and I was absolutely *not* the best golfer there. There were some scratch- and single-digit handicap players in the field, but, that year, I was the best putter. Those greens were all about patience, pace and alignment. Players who were far better than me were four-putting and three-putting the greens and exploding into emotional messes all over the place. I just focused on what I was doing and kept making putts. I was awarded the plaque and my named was engraved on it as that year's champion. (The rotating plaque still hangs somewhere in the magazine's office.)

Interestingly, I learned how my colleagues really felt about me winning our annual event. The next year, they made sure it was scheduled during an LPGA tournament I was supposed to cover. And, I suppose, just to be safe, they also planned for it to be held at the 7,468-yard Bethpage Black Course in Long Island, N.Y. In case you don't know, there is a sign on the first tee of that course that says only highly skilled players should attempt to play Bethpage Black because of its difficulty.

I never played in our company tournament again because it was always scheduled when I was away on assignment. I also began noticing that my male colleagues would sometimes silently disappear together and reappear a few days later – all wearing new golf shirts from places like Pine Valley Country Club, which, by the way, hasn't always rolled out a welcome mat for women.

I knew it wouldn't be easy being the first woman editor at this magazine, but during my recruiting process, I was told they valued my "perspective" and wanted to broaden their scope as a magazine for avid golfers. But I soon noticed sports analogies with things like boxing and football edited into my stories. Why would I ever add into a golf story an analogy to a sport in which the intention is to knock another person unconscious?

I also began to see my male colleagues disappear silently at lunch on Fridays to a private country club to which one of the editors belonged. I had now been left behind to work away in my office with only our editorial assistant, who is female, remaining there with me.

In autumn 1997, I came back to the office after attending the LPGA's annual qualifying tournament in Florida and told my colleagues about this amazing young South Korean player who had just earned her 1998 LPGA Tour card. My colleagues looked at me as if I had grown antlers when I raved about this kid's talent, but in her rookie year the next season, that player –Se Ri Pak – won four tournaments with two major championships.

I also wrote our magazine cover story when Annika Sorenstam became the first woman to score a 59 in an LPGA tournament. Among other memorable highlights, I wrote about players winning career grand slams, played golf in Ireland with LPGA Hall of Famer Patty Sheehan, once interviewed Nancy Lopez in her tournament condo while she cooked my dinner, rode the charter buses and dragged around my share of luggage with LPGA players in Japan, and once, even ran with Karrie Webb through a country club locker room as she attempted to escape a reporter she disliked.

I loved my work, but I felt no team support. Every day was difficult and I felt increasingly more alone. That was less about me winning a silly company golf tournament and more about not fitting into a closed fraternity. There were many days when I simply wanted to return to being a sportswriter at a medium-sized newspaper in a medium-sized town and playing golf once a week with people who didn't eat, sleep and die with this game and their oversized pride in it.

As I read these authors' descriptions of being left behind in their respective offices until they learned to play, I have to admit that I relived that punch-in-the-gut feeling I used to feel on Fridays when everyone disappeared. I learned that I was not alone in that experience.

Conversely, when I read the many stories about women finding accepting colleagues and sharing great camaraderie, I found myself wishing I had experienced that. Golf has positively changed so many of these women's lives! It has given them confidence and helped them improve their business opportunities. I found myself wondering if today's working environment for women professionals in largely male workplaces has, in fact, changed? Their chapters made me hopeful that some workplaces have advanced from the fraternal ostracism I experienced in the golf industry.

Women in these chapters have helped change social paradigms, both in the workplace, as well as in one home nation. There are women who left lucrative positions to follow a dream of working in golf. There are women who doggedly attempted to begin playing the game and can laugh at their own learning curves. Other chapters are about women who used golf to escape great pressures in their jobs, as well as to bond with friends, families and to use the game to market their businesses.

On one hand, these golf stories were worlds apart from the game I have observed and documented for more than two decades, but on the other hand, they were the absolute epitome of what golf truly is when you strip away all the flash, hoopla, money, spotlights, TV cameras, marketing pizzazz and arrogance so often associated with professional golf at the highest level.

These chapters were honest and pure and reminded me of the simple joy I used to feel when I went out on late afternoons to play golf. The game these women described provided flashbacks for me of the smell of turf, the wetness of evening dew and that wonderful clattering ka-plunk of a ball rolling into the cup.

I was inspired and entertained by these women's respective climbs into the game. I laughed out loud as two different authors described wildly errant shots – one, detailing how her ball ricocheted off a man's porch to land at his feet, and another, describing how her pinball golf shot ultimately bathed her friends in potato salad.

That is the true essence of golf – the memories the game provides, the friendship it offers and all of the business benefits that are possible once a foundation of skills are learned.

That is also the common thread that has woven these women together in "Teeing Up For Success," as well as the overall concept of EWGA's membership. It's a large support group of like minded, career focused women who have found a common bond through golf. Together, they have forged a true love of the game in a very personal way.

I'm not sure I'll ever love golf the way I once did. I've often said I'd rather cover excellent golf than play bad golf, but admittedly, I find myself looking at my local courses a little closer these days when I drive by. I watch men change their shoes in the parking lot. I watch women leave the course together, talking excitedly about their rounds.

And the other day, as I passed a local course in the afternoon, I imagined how the grass would feel under my feet or how the wind would hit my face. And, for the first time in a while, I imagined that very satisfying sound a ball makes as it lands on a green and rolls toward the target.

The essence of why you play is a personal experience, but, as I have been reminded by these authors, the reason you play as a group is to share that experience with others and to make memories that last for a lifetime.

About Lisa D. Mickey

Lisa D. Mickey is a veteran golf writer and regular contributor to The New York Times, Virginia Golfer Magazine, usga.org and has served as editor-in-chief of Ladies Links Fore Golf Magazine. She was a former staff writer and associate editor at Golf World Magazine and a former senior editor at Golf For Women Magazine. She was also a senior writer for LPGA.com.

In addition, Lisa co-authored the book "Champions of Women's Golf: Celebrating 50 Years of LPGA Golf," which won the Ben Franklin Book Award in 2001 as the best new recreation/sports book.

In addition, she is a three-time Golf Writers Association of America national winner in feature writing and has also won journalism awards from the Women's Sports Foundation, the North Carolina Press Association and the North Carolina Tennis Association.

Lisa is a native of North Carolina and a current resident of Florida. She earned her undergraduate degree in English at High Point University and studied literature on the graduate level at the University of North Carolina-Greensboro.

Lisa also earned certification as a Florida Master Naturalist through the University of Florida. She currently divides time between golf writing and editing and working as an eco-tour guide on kayaks and a 40-passenger boat through the non-profit Marine Discovery Center in New Smyrna Beach, Fla.

AFTERWORD

We hope these stories will encourage more women to embrace the game of golf. If we've inspired you to take up the game, we invite you to join us. Learn more about EWGA at ewga.com.

Be among the first 500 women to respond to this offer using special promo code EWGA-TeeUp to receive $25 off a new Classic Level member join fee.

We also invite you to share your thoughts about this book with our online community via facebook, LinkedIn or Twitter at:

www.facebook.com/EWGA1

www.linkedin.com/ewga

www.twitter.com/ewga

ABOUT THE EWGA

Founded in 1991 as the Executive Women's Golf Association, the EWGA has enriched the lives of more than 100,000 women through the game of golf. As the largest amateur women's golf organization, the EWGA has Chapters in over 120 cities throughout the United States as well as in international locations including Bermuda, Canada, Italy and South Africa.

EWGA members are primarily working and professional women who share a passion for cultivating relationships and enjoying the game of golf. The association offers a wide range of affordable, organized golf activities and educational programs, social and networking opportunities, discounts and other member benefits. Yet, what members find most valuable are the friendships and relationships made through golf with the EWGA.

EWGA is a tax-exempt 501 (c) 6 membership association. For more information about the EWGA and its membership, visit www.ewga.com

ABOUT THE EWGA FOUNDATION

Established in 2003 as the charitable arm of the EWGA, the mission of the EWGA Foundation is to develop and fund education and leadership programs for women of all ages. Its initiatives include four key areas:

Women On Par® Scholarship program for women ages 30 and older who are interested in beginning or completing their undergraduate college education to get 'on par' with their peers and better themselves both personally and professionally.

Golf Education Curriculum Development & Refinement for EWGA-branded golf learning programs designed to meet the needs of golfers of all skill levels, beginner through more advanced players.

Leadership Development to bring speakers with expertise in leadership development training to EWGA's annual conferences and other public meetings and gatherings.

Financial support and promotion for other charitable organizations whose objectives are aligned with those of the EWGA Foundation. Over the past decade, the EWGA Foundation, through EWGA Chapters and Association-wide fundraising efforts has raised over $500,000 in support of LPGA-USGA Girls Golf.

The EWGA Foundation is a 501(c)(3) charitable not-for-profit organization funded through donations, member contributions and various fundraising activities conducted throughout the year. For more information or to make a donation visit www.ewgafoundation.com.

SPECIAL THANKS AND ACKNOWLEDGEMENTS

The production of this book would not have been possible without the tireless efforts of a dedicated team of women who so generously gave of their time and talents to see this project from inception to publication:

Diana S. Gats
Diana has been an EWGA member since 1999. Since then she has served the organization in many different ways — from local leadership in Canton, OH & Dallas, TX, to her current role as EWGA Association board member. Of all that she has done, her most favorite thing is the EWGA Foundation book project.

"Being the PPP (Persistent, Pain in the Butt, Project Manager) has been a rewarding, insightful, emotional, and incredible experience. EWGA, over the years has motivated me to new business & personal ideas, improved my golf game, and most importantly has brought me my best friends."

Diana is a Business Advisor, Board Facilitator, and speaker. As the President of VPT Enterprise, she works with companies to achieve measureable improvement in their business & their people. She also does LinkedIn training and speaks on Golf for You?

Angie Niehoff
Angie has been actively involved in the association for 20 years, becoming a charter member of the Miami EWGA chapter in 1994 and a Palm Beach County member since 2001. She has served in numerous volunteer roles at the chapter and regional levels as well as six years on the EWGA Association Board. She was an advocate for the formation of the EWGA Foundation and became its first president in 2005. Currently, she is a marketing services consultant for EWGA, serving as a liaison for the National Women's Golf Alliance, the EWGA Foundation Advocates program and international chapter development.

"The EWGA Foundation will always be very dear to my heart and my first charity of choice. For two decades, EWGA has enriched my life with amazing

adventures, experiences and opportunities and an ever expanding network of accomplished women who share my passion for golf and for giving back. It was a joy to work on this book and discover so many fascinating stories."

Angie is President of Niehoff Marketing Associates, providing media relations and marketing services for small businesses and entrepreneurs. Current clients include the Tortuga Rum Cake Company, The Spice Lab, a gourmet sea salt company in the specialty food business, and the EWGA.

Susan J. Snyder
Susan has been a member of EWGA's Palm Beach County, FL chapter since 2006 where she also serves as part of the Association Headquarters staff. In her multifaceted role as director of marketing, Susan's responsibilities include serving as official staff liaison to the EWGA Foundation. Together with EWGA CEO Pam Swensen and with the support of the all-volunteer EWGA Foundation board of directors, Susan manages and coordinates the Foundation's fundraising activities in support of its efforts to enrich women's lives though the game of golf.

"Of all of the fundraising projects the Foundation has undertaken, getting this book project off and running and across the finish line into print has been one of the most personally rewarding. The stories contained within the pages of this book are remarkable accounts of womens' drive to succeed in business – and life – through the game of golf and will inspire readers to tee it up for success."

Pam Swensen
For over 20 years, Pam has been a member of the EWGA. Since becoming the Chief Executive Officer of the organization, she has been impressed and honored to be in the company of so many exceptional women. For her, this book project *"Teeing Up For Success"* has been a true labor of love. Her passion for this association is endless and the inspiring stories in this book depicting the significance golf has played in the lives of 31 women is what the organization is all about. She's certain when the EWGA began 23 years ago, the organization's vision to enrich women's lives through the game of golf seemed unattainable.

"Being involved in this project as an author, team member and as the CEO of this organization, has been an incredibly rewarding experience which is one of my proudest leadership achievements."

SPECIAL THANKS AND ACKNOWLEDGEMENTS, CONTINUED.

Special thanks and sincere appreciation to our chapter authors for sharing their inspiring stories and to all who contributed financially to the production of the EWGA Foundation's, "Teeing up for Success." You are truly remarkable!

Deanna Alfredo
Stacey Baba
Cheri Brennan
Marilyn Bunag
Joan Cavanaugh
Dana Clark, Ph.D.
Thadine Clifton
Margaret E. Downey
Alice Dye
Karen Furtado
Holly Geoghegan
Barbara Gudstadt
Priscilla Hill-Ardoin
Tyra Jarvis
Sheila Johnson
Jacque Jones
Kathy Kolder
Lisa Krouse, Esq., SPHR
Penny Larsen
Christine E. Lynn
Carol Malysz
Karen Moraghan
Kathy O'Neal
Nancy Oliver
Karen Palacios-Jansen
Rosalba Papacostas de Gutierrez
Judy Rankin

Donna Shalala
Mitzi Short
Kim Stanfield
Stina Sternberg
Pam Swensen
Hilary Tuohy
Rita Turner
Debbie Waitkus
Carla Washinko, CPA
B. Camille Williams, MD
Kathy Whitworth

8183108R00131

Made in the USA
San Bernardino, CA
30 January 2014